W9-CDS-647

THIS IS OUR FAITH

THIS IS
OUR FAITH

An Introduction to Catholicism

Thomas P. Rausch, SJ

PAULIST PRESS
New York / Mahwah, NJ

The Scripture quotations contained herein are from the New Revised Standard Version: Catholic Edition Copyright © 1989 and 1993, by the Division of Christian Education of the National Council of the Churches of Christ in the United States of America. Used by permission. All rights reserved.

Cover image by KeilaNeokow EliVokounova / Shutterstock.com
Cover design by Sharyn Banks
Book design by Lynn Else

Copyright © 2014 by Thomas P. Rausch, SJ

All rights reserved. No part of this publication may be reproduced, stored in a retrieval system, or transmitted in any form or by any means, electronic, mechanical, photocopying, recording, scanning, or otherwise, except as permitted under Section 107 or 108 of the 1976 United States Copyright Act, without the prior written permission of the Publisher. Requests to the Publisher for permission should be addressed to the Permissions Department, Paulist Press, 997 Macarthur Boulevard, Mahwah, NJ 07430, (201) 825-7300, fax (201) 825-8345, or online at www.paulistpress.com.

Library of Congress Cataloging-in-Publication Data

Rausch, Thomas P.
    This is our faith : an introduction to Catholicism / Thomas P. Rausch, SJ.
        pages cm
    Includes bibliographical references.
    ISBN 978-0-8091-4893-6 (pbk. : alk. paper) — ISBN 978-1-58768-416-6 (ebook)
    1. Catholic Church—Doctrines. I. Title.
    BX1751.3.R39 2014
    230`.2—dc23
                                                                            2014012785
ISBN 978-0-8091-4893-6 (paperback)
ISBN 978-1-58768-416-6 (e-book)

Published by Paulist Press
997 Macarthur Boulevard
Mahwah, New Jersey 07430

www.paulistpress.com

Printed and bound in the
United States of America

To my students

CONTENTS

Contents

ACKNOWLEDGMENTS

I want to express my deep appreciation to Professor David Wang Xinsheng of Fudan University in Shanghai for his gracious invitation to give a course on Catholicism at Fudan. It was Professor Wang's idea to publish my lectures as a book. I would also like to thank Professor Rachel Zhu Xiaohong of Fudan, who introduced me to the rich culture of Shanghai. I owe a special debt of thanks to Professor Wang's graduate student Liang Jia Rong, who assisted me in many ways during my time in Shanghai and contributed much to the class. And thanks as well to Paul McMahon of Paulist Press for his careful copyediting of the manuscript.

Two chapters were published previously, though in a different form. The section on Pope Benedict XVI originally appeared as an article in *La Civiltà Cattolica*, and the final chapter on Vatican II and global Catholicism appeared in *Chicago Studies*, both in 2013. I'd like to thank Father Antonio Spadaro, SJ, of *La Civiltá Cattolica* and Father Michael Fuller of *Chicago Studies* for permission to include these articles. The graphics were done by Sister Maria Lai, CSJ. I am grateful to all for their help.

ABBREVIATIONS

DOCUMENTS OF VATICAN II

DH   *Dignitatis humanae*: Declaration on Religious Freedom

DV   *Dei verbum*: Dogmatic Constitution on Divine Revelation

GS   *Gaudium et spes*: Pastoral Constitution on the Church in the Modern World

LG   *Lumen gentium*: Dogmatic Constitution on the Church

NA   *Nostra aetate*: Declaration on the Relationship of the Church to Non-Christian Religions

SC   *Sacrosanctum concilium*: Constitution on the Sacred Liturgy

UR   *Unitatis redintegratio*: Decree on Ecumenism

OTHER

CDF   Congregation of the Doctrine of the Faith

DI   *Dominus Iesus*

DS   Denzinger-Schönmetzer, *Enchiridion Symbolorum*, 33rd ed. (Freiburg: Herder, 1965).

INTRODUCTION

This book began as a course taught in China at Fudan University in Shanghai in the summer of 2013. Asked to introduce the students to contemporary Catholicism, most of whom had a basic familiarity with Christianity but were not themselves Christians and had little knowledge of Catholicism, I structured it around the basic articles of the Apostles' Creed. This ancient summary of the faith of the church goes back to the end of the second century, originally the interrogatory creed of the church in Rome, confessed in the baptism of neophytes and already called the *Apostles Creed* (*symbolum apostolorum*) in a letter sent by the Synod of Milan to Pope Siricius in 390.

While not on the creed itself,[1] the trinitarian nature of the creed suggested the structure for the course: God, Jesus, the Spirit, and the church. Thus we begin with the question of the Divine Mystery, looking briefly at various efforts to image the Divine on the part of ancient peoples, who ended mostly constructing their gods in their own image before moving to the mysterious, transcendent God of the Judeo-Christian tradition, an incomprehensible God who lives in unapproachable light. At the same time, this God is confessed as having created humankind in the Divine Image and Likeness and entering into a personal relationship with his creatures.

From there we move to Jesus, the Word of God and Son through whom the transcendent God breaks the silence of the ages and reveals himself by living among us. A following chapter on Christology looks at the efforts of the early Christian communities to interpret the Jesus story, drawing on Old Testament images and the writings of the evangelists.

Next we take up the Spirit, personifying God's creative presence in the Old Testament, empowering Jesus in his historical ministry, gathering a people holy to the Lord, and giving us communion in the Divine Mystery revealed as Father, Son, and Spirit. This introduces the mystery of the Trinity.

Then we turn to the portrait of the church in the New Testament, the images or metaphors that describe its nature, the growth of the New Testament communities into a church, called *catholic* as early as 110 by Ignatius of Antioch, an early bishop and martyr. Protestant scholars often call this process *early Catholicism*, for them a negative, though it gave the church the institutional form that has enabled it to survive as a community for two millennia. We conclude the section by considering the church's two foundational sacraments, baptism and Eucharist.

The final section of the course and this book focuses on contemporary Catholicism. The Second Vatican Council, one of three great reforming movements in the church's history, was an effort to renew and update the Catholic Church, in many ways bringing it into the modern world and committing it to the search for Christian unity. We consider some of its more important documents and decrees that set the agenda for what is now the third millennium of the church's life. Another chapter looks at two of the most recent popes, Benedict XVI and Francis, the first pope from the global South, where most Catholics today live. A final chapter looks at the phenomenon of global Catholicism.

My hope is that this book will provide a popular introduction to Catholicism. While it is based on good scholarship, I want the book to be easy to read and digest. Thus I have tried to keep the chapters short and footnotes to a bare minimum.

NOTE

1. For example, Thomas P. Rausch, *I Believe in God: A Reflection on the Apostles' Creed* (Collegeville, MN: Liturgical Press, 2008).

PART I

God the Father Almighty

CHAPTER I

A GOD BEYOND IMAGES

In his massive work *A Secular Age*, Charles Taylor traces the gradual stripping of Western civilization of its mystery, its narratives of faith and religious practice, and ultimately its eschatological hope.[1] He sees the process of abolishing the enchanted medieval cosmos as beginning with the Reformation, with its emphasis on personal faith and its discomfort with sacraments, priesthood, and the sacred, leading eventually toward the creation of a humanist alternative to faith. The Enlightenment saw a slide toward the impersonal, with increasingly secular modernity substituting Deism and Unitarianism for historic Christianity. God was no longer interacting in history with human beings and the created order but had been replaced by an impersonal architect whose indifferent universe was governed by unchanging natural laws. From this perspective, Taylor argues that Deism can be seen as a "half-way house" on the road to contemporary atheism.[2]

This loss of a sense for the transcendent meant that spirituality increasingly became focused, not on God, but on the self, on personal feelings; thus it was privatized and opposed to religion, which was now seen as institutional and impersonal.[3] God had become an impersonal principle, or a "higher power"; think of contemporary New Age spiritualities or "the Force" of the movie series "Star Wars." Many people mixed and matched beliefs, claiming they were "spiritual but not religious."

But the Divine Mystery cannot be completely banished from creation; it has a way of manifesting itself, intruding unexpectedly into our consciousness in moments of disclosure or revelation, like Freud's return of the repressed. Many of us have had the experience of intuiting something more, a sense of graciousness in the world, a sense of wonder, even of presence, sometimes triggered by nature or a gift of love or even stress.

How do we come to understand and describe this irruption of the transcendent, the Divine Mystery we call God, into the realm of our awareness? How can we grasp this mystery in its otherness, without reducing it to some figment of our imagination or psychological projection?

IMAGES OF THE DIVINE

How we conceptualize the Divine is enormously important, for inadequate images or naive concepts can become obstacles to an encounter with the One that remains beyond our imagining. It is true that human beings from time immemorial have created gods in their own image, projecting their insecurities and dreams on to an all-powerful other or others. The ancients worshiped natural forces or malevolent demons, the spirits of their ancestors, or the gods of their individual city-states. Sometimes their gods were philosophical principles rather than personal deities.

MYTHOLOGIES

Thus the inhabitants of ancient Mesopotamia and Canaan ritualized the fertility of nature, so important in their arid environment, with elaborate rituals that involved sexual intercourse between the god and his consort, symbolized by the temple priest and priestess, and with all those present sharing in the ritual. Some practiced human sacrifice. The gods of Mesoamerica were bloodthirsty deities whose cults often involved human sacrifice. It is believed that more than a thousand victims a day were sacrificed over a period of twenty days when the sixth temple of the Temple Mayor in Tenochtitlan, the Aztec capital of what is now Mexico City, was dedicated in 1487. The gods of Greek and Roman mythologies were anthropomorphic deities, idealized human figures who governed the heavens, the seas, and the under-world, or alternatively personifications of natural forces such as love or war. Their veneration was supposed to provide some protection from powers beyond human control. Neither transcendent nor "holy" in the sense of "righteous," these mythological deities were as capricious as the human beings whose virtues and more often vices they reflected. They were gods created in the image of man, rather than man created in the image of God, as in the biblical view.

ULTIMATE PRINCIPLE

Other notions of the Divine were philosophically conceived. Traditional Chinese deities mirrored the stratified, hierarchical nature of imperial Chinese society or were conceived as manifestations of the one Dao. As described by the legendary Chinese philosopher Lao Tzu, the Dao exists before the entire universe and generates the myriad things in the world, making it the "mother of the universe." The Dao itself is nameless, eternal, ineffable, unchanging, the source of being; it depends on nothing and cannot be represented.[4] Thus the Dao is the ultimate principle, though it remains impersonal. The Dao does not come to us; we must go to the Dao.

Similarly, the ancient Greeks sought to identify the ultimate principle (*archē*) of all that is. Plato's God was a *noûs* or intellect eternally contemplating the forms, though his ultimate principle seems to have been the Idea of the Good, which is the source of all the forms. The God of Aristotle was a self-enclosed deity, described as pure thought thinking itself. Neither creator nor personal, Aristotle's deity was a spiritual being, pure and changeless, an eternal, cosmological cause or prime mover, posited to explain the world's motion but without contact with it.[5] In David Knowles's words, "As his own being is the only fit object for his contemplation he has no knowledge of, or care for, the individual, and the whole machinery of the world is set and kept in motion by the love and desire that all being, consciously or unconsciously, has for God."[6] The idea of a personal God who might reach out to human beings in love and communion did not occur to the ancients.

A PERSONAL GOD

Fundamental to the Abrahamic religious traditions is the idea of a personal God entering into relationship with humankind. In other words, ultimate reality is not a force of nature or a philosophical principle. Still less can it be reduced to electrons, protons, and neutrons, the submicroscopic reality of the physicist. Ultimate reality is personal, or as Pope Benedict XVI phrased it, reason (*logos*; cf. John 1:1–3) and love, the source of all that is, the source of being itself.[7] God's very nature is to communicate himself.

These monotheistic religions originated in the Middle East, starting with Israel's experience of God. The God of the patriarchs delivered the children of Israel from bondage and entered into an exclusive covenant relationship with them: "I, the Lord, am your God, who brought you out of the land of Egypt, that place of slavery. You shall not have other gods besides me" (Exod 20:2–3). Israel's often troubled but passionate relationship with that God who its people called Yahweh, a name derived from the root *hayah*, "to be," in Exodus 3:14, is reflected in the books of the Old Testament, composed over some thousand years of Jewish history.

This same God for Christians took on flesh in the person of Jesus, God's Word (John 1:1) and only begotten Son who poured out his blood for the salvation of the world. The doctrine of the Trinity, with its roots in the New Testament, teaches that relationality lies at the very heart of the Divine Mystery. The compassionate God of Islam, for Muslims closer to the believer than his jugular vein, is a God who has spoken his final word in the holy Qur'an, revealed through the prophet Mohammad.

MODERN DEATH OF GOD

But modernity subjected that personal God of the great monotheistic traditions to a transformation or metamorphosis. Under the influence of the German idealists, the Divine Mystery was again depersonalized, reduced to an alienated personification of spirit, mind, or human intelligence. Hegel (1770–1831) taught that the object of religion was an Absolute Being that comes from and was produced by human consciousness itself.[8] Consequently, religious belief was self-estrangement or self-alienation, to be overcome through the enlightenment of pure insight in which self-consciousness recognized the infinite object of belief as itself. Feuerbach (1804–72) learned from Hegel, adopting his concept of alienation and naturalizing his Absolute into an objectified projection of human self-consciousness. Religion was the self-alienation and self-objectification of the human person into an external, absolute deity.[9] Humans negate themselves to create a God. Hegel's Absolute was humanity's real, unrecognized essence, a projection of human psychology.[10] In this sense, Feuerbach was the progenitor of both Marx and Freud. God was humanity's own projected need.

If primitive mythologies anthropomorphized the Divine and modernity psychologized it away, with Nietzsche (1844–1900) a new theme emerges. In his *Die fröhliche Wissenschaft*, he sees the death of God as a deliberate decision, symbolic of modernity: "Where is God?" Nietzsche's Madman asks. "I tell you! We have killed him—you and I! We are all his murderers."[11]

> How shall we console ourselves, the murderers of all murderers! The holiest and the mightiest thing the world has ever possessed has bled to death under our knives: who will wipe the blood from us? With what water could we cleanse ourselves? What festivals of atonement, what holy games will we have to invent for ourselves? Is the magnitude of this deed not too great for us? Do we not ourselves have to become gods merely to appear worthy of it?[12]

In his study *The Death of God*, Frederiek Depoortere traces a line from Luther through Hegel to Nietzsche, suggesting, like Taylor, a link between Protestantism and modern atheism.[13] The death of God means a loss of transcendence, and with it, the loss of any absolute or universal morality.[14] One thinks immediately of the remark first attributed to Dostoyevsky in *The Brothers Karamazov* by Jean Paul Sartre, "If there is no God, everything is permitted." Advances in science such as Darwin's doctrine of evolution through natural selection and Einstein's argument for a closed, deterministic universe have also made belief in a personal God more difficult.

In more recent times, a group of popular writers known

collectively as the "new atheists" have taken on God and religion, especially Christianity, with a vengeance. Foremost among them are Richard Dawkins, Sam Harris, and the late Christopher Hitchens, though they are not the only ones. While they have sold a good number of books, their arguments, based on a type of naive scientism that seeks to submit religious claims to empirical verification as though God were an object in the world, have been faulted by their critics for failing to address the theological tradition on a serious level. We have already seen at the beginning of this chapter that the Judeo-Christian understanding of God is a transcendent God beyond being, or better, a God that is being itself, pure self-subsistence. This transcendent God can never be an object in the world, to be apprehended like other beings. It cannot be sensed, perceived, even understood, for the Divine Mystery is "incomprehensible."

Indeed, as John Haught argues, the "engagement with theology on the part of these 'new atheists' lies at about the same level of reflection on faith that one can find in contemporary creationist and fundamentalist literature."[15] Richard Dawkins arguing that the notion of God should be treated like any other scientific hypothesis or Sam Harris wondering why a book like the Bible, supposedly "authored by the Creator of the universe," would not be the richest source of mathematical insight available shows them to be profoundly ignorant of the philosophical tradition. Richard Gaillardetz characterizes these new atheists as presupposing a "naïve form of theism" that perceives God as just another individual being, albeit the Supreme Being.[16] In this they are no different from the ancients whose idea of the Divine was simply a more powerful being or beings, perhaps changeless or eternal, but still a this-worldly deity, not a transcendent God who is "wholly other."

DIVINE TRANSCENDENCE

The great lesson of the biblical tradition, expressed in many different ways, is the otherness or transcendence of God. This is a God very different from the mythological deities of ancient civilizations. As the Psalmist says with sarcasm in God's name, "I will not accept a bull from your house, or goats from your folds....Do I eat the flesh of bulls or drink the blood of goats?" (Ps 50:9, 13). This God is different from the abstract and impersonal first principle of the philosophers. Nor can this God be reduced to a scientific hypothesis or to a projection of human hopes. Israel's God is a God who remains mystery even in relationship, beyond our imagining or even our understanding, and yet a God whose presence is intuited, grasped prior to concepts in our sense for the absolute that is Truth, Beauty, and the source of all things that are. To gain an insight into the mystery of the Divine, we need to consider first God's transcendence.

ISRAEL'S GOD

The transcendence of Israel's God, beyond images, dwelling apart, dangerous even to gaze upon, is suggested in the Hebrew Scriptures by the notion of God as holy. The idea of holiness (from the Hebrew root *qds*, "separate") emphasizes God's otherness, difference, or apartness from all that is created, limited, and imperfect; it is a constant in the Old Testament. Even the holy name of God, YHWH, was not to be pronounced. In other words, God is the transcendent, the "wholly other" (*totaliter aliter*), the holy, what Rudolf Otto calls *das Heilige*, the *mysterium tremendum et fascinans*, the Mystery that is both terrifying and fascinating.[17] Some biblical examples might include Moses standing in awe on holy ground before the burning bush (Exod 3:2–6) or Elijah hiding in the cave, discerning the Mystery not in dramatic displays of power but in a tiny whispering voice (1 Kgs 19:9–13).

The Book of Job teaches that even for the just man who fears God and avoids evil (Job 1:1), God remains a mystery, beyond our ability to understand. When Job is struck by a series of tragedies, leaving him without wealth, family, or health, his friends gather around, urging him to acknowledge his guilt. But Job is steadfast in maintaining his innocence. Finally, when he demands an answer of God, challenging in effect the popular view that God punishes the wicked and rewards the just with prosperity, God answers Job out of the whirlwind in some of the most beautiful poetry in the Old Testament:

> "Who is this that darkens counsel by words without
>   knowledge?
> Gird up your loins like a man,
>   I will question you, and you shall declare to me.
>
> "Where were you when I laid the foundation of the
>   earth?
>   Tell me, if you have understanding.
> Who determined its measurements—surely you know!
>   Or who stretched the line upon it?
> On what were its bases sunk,
>   or who laid its cornerstone
> when the morning stars sang together
>   and all the heavenly beings shouted for joy?
>
> "Or who shut in the sea with doors
>   when it burst out from the womb?—
> when I made the clouds its garment,
>   and thick darkness its swaddling band,

and prescribed bounds for it,
    and set bars and doors,
and said, 'Thus far shall you come, and no farther,
    and here shall your proud waves be stopped'?

"Have you commanded the morning since your days
      began,
    and caused the dawn to know its place,
so that it might take hold of the skirts of the earth,
    and the wicked be shaken out of it?

....

"Can you bind the chains of the Pleiades,
    or loose the cords of Orion?
Can you lead forth the Mazzaroth in their season,
    or can you guide the Bear with its children?
Do you know the ordinances of the heavens?
    Can you establish their rule on the earth?"
                            (Job 38:2–13; 31–33)

The answer Job receives to his *crie du coeur* points to the mysteries of creation and its creator, far beyond our understanding, suggesting powerfully the divine incomprehensibility.

In another charming story, Moses, who enjoyed an intimate relationship with God (Exod 33:11), is not able to see God's face, for according to the biblical tradition, so different from our Western tendency to domesticate the Divine, no one can look upon the face of God and live (Exod 33:20; cf. Judg 13:22). However, God makes an exception for Moses. Placing him in the hollow of the rock, God covers Moses protectively with his hand and passes by "so that you may see my back, but my face is not to be seen" (Exod 33:18–23).

The story suggests that we get only glimpses of God, insights into the Divine Mystery that remains incomprehensible.

These two stories express an enduring paradox, that God is both transcendent (other) and immanent (close). The word *holy* refers to God's otherness, difference, or apartness from created reality, which by definition is limited and imperfect. The Decalogue or Ten Commandments forbade representation of God by images "of anything in the sky above or on the earth below or in the waters beneath the earth" (Exod 20:3; cf. Deut 5:8). God dwells in an impenetrable "cloud" (Exod 20:21; 24:15). No images of Israel's God have ever been found; nor did their God, like the gods of the nations that surrounded them, have a sexual partner or enter into sexual relations with humans like the gods of the Greeks and Romans.

The Islamic tradition inherited from the Jewish Scriptures this prohibition of images, teaching that the transcendent God can never be identified with created reality; to do so is to commit the unforgivable sin. Christianity, however, with its foundation in the doctrine of the incarnation, the incredible belief that God became man in the person of Jesus, sees humanity as capable of embodying and even imaging the Divine, something seen most clearly in the Catholic tradition's appreciation of the power of nature, art, and symbol as mediating the Divine Mystery, what has been described as its sacramental imagination.[18]

There was also a strong moral dimension to the Israelite experience of God, who commanded, "Be holy, for I the LORD your God am holy" (Lev 19:2). In other words, God's people were to be "set apart," unlike others, "holy" as their God was holy. Thus they struggled against any religious syncretism, did not practice child sacrifice as some ancient peoples in Canaan seem to have done, and refused to take part in the fertility cults of their neighbors. This was a God who could never sanction violence, as Pope Benedict XVI argued in his controversial Regensburg address.

GOD IN CHRISTIAN THEOLOGY

The Hebrew sense for God's otherness or transcendence is also reflected in the Christian tradition. For the New Testament author of 1 Timothy, God "dwells in unapproachable light" (6:16) that blinds the eyes of our understanding—a metaphor that appears often in the tradition. Gregory of Nyssa, a fourth-century church father, described the soul, seeking to contemplate the Divine Mystery, as entering into a "luminous darkness." The soul "keeps on going deeper until by the operation of the spirit it penetrates the invisible and incomprehensible, and it is there that it seeks God. The true vision and the true knowledge of what we seek consists precisely in not seeing, in an awareness that our goal transcends all knowledge and is everywhere cut off from us by the darkness of incomprehensibility."[19]

Anselm of Canterbury, an eleventh-century monk, theologian, and bishop, uses metaphorical language to compare the light in which God dwells to the sun, blinding the human intellect, just as we risk blindness by gazing directly at the sun:

> Surely, Lord, inaccessible light is your dwelling place, for no one apart from yourself can enter into it and fully comprehend you. If I fail to see this light it is simply because it is too bright for me. Still, it is by this light that I do see all that I can, even as weak eyes, unable to look straight at the sun, see all that they can be the sun's light.[20]

A fourteenth-century English mystic described contemplative prayer as an entering into a "cloud of unknowing," while John of the Cross, a sixteenth-century Spanish poet and mystic described this experience as the "dark night," blinding both the senses and the intellect.

Thomas Aquinas (1225–74), known in the West as the Angelic Doctor, described a God who was pure act, whose very nature was "to be."

> Now God's action is not limited by any agent, because it proceeds from no other but himself: nor is it limited by any recipient, because since there is no passive potency in him, he is pure self-subsistent act....The being of God, since it is not received into anything, but is pure being, is not limited to any particular mode of a perfection of being, but contains all being within itself: and thus as being taken in its widest sense can extend to an infinity of things, so the divine being is infinite: and hence it is clear that his might or active power is infinite.[21]

Unlike created beings, which have being only by participation, God, for Aquinas, is pure subsistent Being, pure existence. God's essence and existence are the same.[22] Thus, "God is neither a species nor an individual, nor is there difference in him. Nor can he be defined, since every definition is taken from the genus and species."[23] Etienne Gilson uses the word *aseity* (from the Latin, *a se*, "by itself") to describe this unique way of existing without cause. Such a God was not just another being, albeit an all-powerful one. God's very essence is to be, the source of all that is.[24] This is a God that no idea or image could adequately represent; it is not an anthropologically conceived or psychologically projected idea of God, but the incomprehensible, unknowable, transcendent God of Judaism and Christianity. The very nature of God as pure existence is to be active, to give existence, to create, to gift or endow. The Scholastics used to say, in God, *esse est agere*; that is, "to be is to act." God is not a being among others in the world, the mistake of the new atheists; God is Being itself, pure, dynamic existence.

In his later years, the great German theologian Karl Rahner began to speak about the incomprehensibility (*Unbegreiflichkeit*) of God. Basing his argument on the teaching of Aquinas, he maintained that the disparity between the infinite being of God and the finite human intellect was so great that even in the beatific vision—the immediate vision of God to which we look forward in faith—God cannot be comprehended or understood.[25] Not one being among others, God is absolute being, the "holy mystery" that we cannot experience directly as we can other things in the world. Even to speak about God is difficult, for God remains ineffable, nameless, and unknowable. god = personal

We grasp this mystery only through analogies drawn from our experience; God is a person, therefore self-aware, loving, and free. We call God "father," "shepherd," "king," "Lord," the "ground of our being," or simply "Thou." If we can know something about God by analogy and especially through revelation, the distance between what we can know and the Divine Mystery remains infinitely greater. In fact, Rahner argues, in the beatific vision God's incomprehensibility actually increases because the beatific vision reveals God's absolute simplicity as pure, subsistent being (*ipsum esse subsistens*).

Thus, to speak about the divine incomprehensibility is really to refer to the finite, limited character of human knowing, something medieval theologians understood. This concept of God as pure subsistent being, absolutely simple, incomprehensible, is one of the great treasures of Christian theology. Pope Benedict appeals to the experience of the great mystics for whom God "is not seen...but is experienced as one who acts and who remains (for the inner as for the outer eye) in the dark."[26]

CONCLUSION

We have seen in this opening chapter that the idea of God that comes out of the Judeo-Christian tradition is radically different from the gods of the nations. Neither a personification of a force of nature, nor a demonic figure demanding the blood of the innocent, nor an idealized human being, nor a philosophical principle without interiority or relationship, this God of the Bible lies beyond our power to imagine or comprehend, paradoxically dwelling in darkness or inaccessible light.

While the gods of the ancients were deities constructed in the image and likeness of human beings, the God of the Bible is a God who creates human beings in the divine image and likeness (Gen 1:26–27). Aquinas and the Scholastics of the Middle Ages saw this God not as a being among others but as Being itself, pure act or existence, the cause of all that is.

At the same time, fundamental to Israel's experience is that this transcendent God is also immanent, close, and personal. This is a God who desires to communicate and to be in relationship. This is a God who has both a face and a name. In the early Israelite writings, particularly those of the Jahwist tradition, going back to the ninth century BCE, God is described in anthropomorphic terms. God reveals his mysterious name to Moses as Yahweh, translated as "I am who I am" (Exod 3:14), with its mysterious association with absolute being or existence. How this incomprehensible, transcendent God, who is also immanent, overcomes the divine otherness and becomes the God of a people is the subject of our next chapter.

NOTES

1. Charles Taylor, *A Secular Age* (Cambridge, MA: The Belknap Press of Harvard University Press, 2007).

2. Ibid., 77, 270.

3. Ibid., 505–35.

4. JeeLoo Liu, *An Introduction to Chinese Philosophy* (Malden, MA: Blackwell Publishing, 2006), 135–37.

5. See Alexander Sissel Kohanski, *The Greek Mode of Thought in Western Philosophy* (Rutherford, NJ: Fairleigh Dickenson University Press, 1984), 66–70; cf. Aristotle, Meta. 1072 a. 24.

6. David Knowles, *The Evolution of Medieval Thought*, 2nd ed. (London: Longman, 1988), 12–13.

7. Joseph Ratzinger, *Church, Ecumenism and Politics* (New York: Crossroad, 1988), 152–53; *Deus caritas est, no. 10.*

8. G. W. F. Hegel, *The Phenomenology of Mind*, intro. George Lichtheim (New York: Harper Torchbooks, 1967), 567; see Robert Tucker, *Philosophy and Myth in Karl Marx*, 2nd ed. (Cambridge [EN]: At the University Press, 1972), 39–44.

9. Tucker, *Philosophy and Myth in Karl Marx*, 85–94.

10. See Sidney Hook, *From Hegel to Marx: Studies in the Intellectual Development of Karl Marx* (New York: Columbia University Press, 1994), 220–30, 248–50; see also Henri De Lubac, *The Drama of Atheist Humanism* (Cleveland: World Publishing Company, 1963), 7–17.

11. Friedrich Nietzsche, *The Gay Science*, ed. Bernard Williams (Cambridge: Cambridge University Press, 2001), no. 125.

12. Ibid.

13. See "Luther, Hegel and the Death of God," in Frederiek Depoortere, *The Death of God: An Investigation into the History of the Western Concept of God* (London: T & T Clark, 2008), 153–74.

14. Ibid., 22.

15. John F. Haught, *God and the New Atheism: A Critical Response to Dawkins, Harris and Hitchens* (Louisville, KY: Westminster John Knox Press, 2008), xi; see also Peter Steinfels,

"The New Atheism, and Something More," *The New York Times* (February 13, 2009); http://www.nytimes.com/2009/02/14/us/14 beliefs.html.

16. Richard R. Gaillardetz, "Catholicism and the New Atheism," *America* (May 5, 2008).

17. Rudolf Otto, *The Idea of the Holy* (New York: Oxford University Press, 1958).

18. See John Pfordresher, *Jesus and the Emergence of a Catholic Imagination* (New York: Paulist, 2008); also Thomas P. Rausch, "The Catholic Imagination," in *Being Catholic in a Culture of Choice* (Collegeville, MN: Liturgical Press, 2006), 20–35.

19. Gregory of Nyssa, *Life of Moses*, no. 163.

20. Anselm, *Proslogion*, 16.

21. Aquinas, *De Potentia Dei*, q. 1, art 2, trans. the English Dominican Fathers (Westminster, MD: The Newman Press, 1952, reprint of 1932).

22. Ibid, q. 7, art. 2.

23. Ibid., q. 7, art. 3.

24. See Etienne Gilson, *The Spirit of Medieval Philosophy* (New York: Charles Scribner's Sons, 1936).

25. Karl Rahner, "Thomas Aquinas on the Incomprehensibility of God," *Journal of Religion* 58 Supplement (1978): S107–25.

26. Joseph Ratzinger, *Truth and Tolerance: Christian Belief and World Religions* (San Francisco: Ignatius Press, 2004), 42.

CHAPTER 2

A PERSONAL GOD

THE GOD OF THE BIBLE

From the beginning, the transcendent God of the Bible is a God who has been reaching out to humankind, created in the divine image and likeness (Gen 1:27). As an icon for this chapter, we might consider Michelangelo's wonderful work "The Creation of Adam," adorning the roof of the Sistine Chapel in the Vatican. In it, God, borne by the angels, reaches out to his magnificent creature, Adam—which in Hebrew means both man and woman—while Adam extends his hand toward God. Their gazes meet, but their hands do not quite touch, symbolizing the distance that remains between the creature and the creator; yet they are so close. This is a God who wants to be in relationship.

Thus, the God of the Bible is a God who is seeking to enter into relationship with humankind. This is a God who communicates, breaking the silence of his otherness and transcendence, speaking the divine word into space and time in his great work of creation and later addressing his people through the prophetic figures like Moses, Nathan, Elijah, Isaiah, and ultimately Jesus, who speak in the divine name. The word of the Lord becomes a key concept, and in Jesus, the Word of God has become flesh. The story of God's relationship with humankind begins with the story of creation.

A GOD WHO CREATES

The first eleven chapters of the Book of Genesis, set at the beginning of the Pentateuch by the fifth-century Priestly editors, serve as a kind of overture to the biblical narratives that follow. They include stories of the creation, the fall, and the fratricide, sin, and social chaos that follow upon the man's and the woman's rejecting God in the effort to become gods themselves. The Book of Genesis actually has two creation stories: the first from the Priestly editors (Gen 1:1—2:4a) and the second from the Jahwist tradition (Gen 2:4b–25), so called because it uses the divine name JHWH/Lord anachronistically, long before God reveals it to Moses. Israelite authors borrowed the basic narrative of the first creation story from the Babylonian epic known as the *Enuma Elish*. But they changed it significantly.

Enuma Elish, Table IV, 135–40	Genesis 1:6–7
Then the lord paused to view her dead body, That he might divide the monster and do artful works. He split her like a shellfish into two parts: Half of her he set up and ceiled it as sky, Pulled down the bar and posted guards. He bade them to allow not her waters to escape.	And God said, "Let there be a dome in the midst of the waters, and let it separate the waters from the waters." So God made the dome and separated the waters that were under the dome from the waters that were above the dome.

While a literalist reading of these opening chapters of Genesis represents a decidedly unmodern credulity, with its stories of creation in seven days, a tempting serpent in a garden of innocence, an escape from the great flood on an ark loaded with all the animals of the earth, and a tower aimed at the heavens, a more sophisticated reflection reveals at least four highly suggestive themes. They are rich in religious meaning:

1. *Creation*: God overcomes primordial chaos to create the heavens and the earth and all that is in them. Creation is good, the work of God's hands. The implication is that evil does not come from the creator, but from somewhere else.

2. *Dignity of Humankind*: Man and woman are created in the image and likeness of God, grounding the intrinsic dignity and value of each human being. The Catholic respect for all human life, from the unborn to the prisoner on death row to the elderly or the homeless, is rooted here; each person is of absolute value, created in the image and likeness of God. All are created in freedom, equality, and for one another; there is no subordination of one to the other. They are destined for intimacy with God, who comes to walk with them in the cool of the evening, and there is an innocence about them; they are "naked" and not ashamed.

3. *The Fall*: Original innocence is lost when the couple succumbs to the temptation of the serpent, which is much more than mere disobedience. The temptation is subtle—to become like gods themselves, which means to choose autonomy rather than their status as creatures; they would no longer have to acknowledge God, the perennial temptation. Sin—the Hebrew word means "to miss the mark," "to fail to reach one's goal"—ruptures the original harmonious relationship among the couple and God, nature,

and themselves. What follows is murder, strife, the near destruction of the earth through the flood, and the division of humanity through the dividing of their languages—all these are the results of sin. Sin threatens to bring about the destruction of God's creative work, an even more real possibility in our world today.

4. *Salvation*: God's will is always to save. In spite of the chaos that this first (original) sin lets back into the world, God intervenes constantly to save, giving the man and woman clothes to cover their nakedness, marking Cain to protect him from Abel's vengeful tribe, delivering Noah and humankind from the waters of the flood, and promising a blessing in which all nations will share.

A GOD IN HISTORY

The God who creates the heavens and the earth is also a God active in history. We see this a few chapters later in the story of the call of the patriarch Abraham and God's promise to make of his descendants a great nation through whom all the peoples of the earth would be blessed (Gen 12:1–3). Thus, mythology gives way to history, with the promise of a fulfillment yet to come.

> Now the LORD said to Abram, "Go from your country and your kindred and your father's house to the land that I will show you. I will make of you a great nation, and I will bless you, and make your name great, so that you will be a blessing. I will bless those who bless you, and the one who curses you I will

curse; and in you all the families of the earth shall be blessed." (Gen 12:1–3)

What follows in succeeding chapters and books of the Old Testament is the biblical metanarrative of the working out of God's promise through prophetic figures and saving acts in history on behalf of his people. It combines Israel's history with a religious interpretation through a rereading of events in the life of the nation. God delivers the children of Israel from slavery in Egypt, entering into a special "covenant" relationship with them, giving them the Ten Commandments, and leading them with mighty deeds into the land of promise, Israel. When they are unfaithful to the terms of the covenant, he sends prophets to warn them of his coming judgment but also continues to promise that he will not abandon them.

In the later history of Israel, after they survive a period of exile in Babylon, the expectation grows of some new, even definitive intervention by Yahweh God. The messianic tradition uses many and varied poetic images to portray the hope of God's coming salvation, including that of the Son of David, or "anointed" Messiah, sometimes called the Son of God. The later Wisdom tradition wrestles with the question of why it is that the just, rather than the wicked, are the ones who suffer, and it raises the question of God's wisdom, Sophia, coming into the world. The apocalyptic tradition raises the hope that one day or on the last day God will raise the dead to life. Christians, of course, see this long narrative of a saving history fulfilled in the story of Jesus, the Son of God and Word of the Father.

THE GOD OF CHRISTIANITY

While the Christian tradition grows out of the faith of Israel and the Hebrew Scriptures, called by Christians the

Old Testament, its perspective is different. The New Testament understands Jesus as the Son of God, who has come into the world to make the Father known, who lays down his life in faithfulness to his mission of proclaiming God's kingdom or reign, and who is glorified or raised up to the Father's right hand. The doctrine of the Trinity, rooted in the New Testament but formulated later in the history of the church, is further evidence of the personal nature of God. God is not just revealed in history as Father, Son, and Spirit (what theologians call the economic Trinity), but the one God exists as a unity of three relations or "persons," to use the technical theological term: "God...simply does not exist except as three persons. Vice versa, the divine persons are not other than the divine *ousia*, they are the *ousia*."[1] In other words, God is not just personal but intersubjective; relationality is at the very heart of the Christian understanding of the Divine Mystery.

If the Judeo-Christian experience of the Divine gives us a God who is personal, it was precisely the influence of Christianity, specifically the efforts of the church fathers of the first Christian centuries, to formulate the Christian experience of God as Father, Son, and Spirit that moved Western culture and philosophy to a new level of understanding. Walter Kasper argues that the Cappodocian distinction between one nature (*ousia*) and three *hypostases* (substance, being), understood as the concrete realization of a universal nature, introduced a new ontological category. Even if hypostasis was not yet understood as person in the psychological sense, it meant "nothing less than that the universal nature was no longer regarded as the supreme reality and that the Greek ontological way of thinking was giving way to thinking in terms of persons."[2] Christians see persons as different from other beings, because they are free, able to love and to create, capable of producing beauty and truth.

Each person is a value in him- or herself, never to be used as a mere means to something else.

Or to put it another way, rather than seeing universal nature—Plato's forms or Aristotle's universals—as the supreme reality, under the influence of Christianity, the most real henceforth would be seen as the existing individual *hypostasis*/substance, and ultimately, as personal.

KNOWING THE TRANSCENDENT GOD

When it comes to the question of how we can know the transcendent God, Protestant and Catholic theologies have responded differently. Protestant theology, heavily influenced by an Augustinian emphasis on the corruption of human nature due to original sin, has limited knowledge of God to what is learned from direct revelation, thus to Scripture. Catholic theological anthropology, more positive, admits of some knowledge of the Divine apart from revelation. To explore this more fully, we need to consider the different roles of natural theology, revelation, the relation of faith and reason, and theology itself.

NATURAL THEOLOGY

Natural theology approaches the question of God and God's existence in light of reason alone; thus it is a properly philosophical discipline rather than a theological one based on revelation. A classic example would be the "five ways" of Thomas Aquinas, a thirteenth-century theologian and doctor of the church. Aquinas offers five "ways" or arguments to "prove" the existence of God, arguments from motion, efficient causality, contingency, from the grades of perfection in all things, and from design or order, often called teleology.[3] While these arguments offer evidence for God's existence, they are not demonstrative in the ways that a scientific argument would prove its conclusions. Rather, they offer reasons convincing to some, not to others. Perhaps most convincing is Aquinas's argument from contingency.

Aquinas stressed the difference between God as subsistent being—being without cause—and contingent beings, which have being only by participation. In the words of Robert Barron, "[What] comes forth from God is utterly of God, yet, as finite and created, it is finitely other than God, so that the integrity of creation is a function of its absolute dependency upon the Creator."[4] Thus created beings are beings only in an analogous sense, which sets up what the tradition has called the analogy of being (*analogia entis*).

The analogy of being means that while God remains transcendent, there is an analogy, commonality, even communion between God's pure existence and the beings of the world that grounds the possibility of metaphysical knowledge, the divine immanence, and ultimately, what the Catholic tradition speaks of as the sacramental imagination. Catholic theology believes that because of the analogy of being, humans can know *that* God exists, though, of course, personal knowledge of God depends on revelation. At the same time, Catholic theology stresses that grace builds on nature. It recognizes that human intelligence continually reaches beyond the things that are directly experienced to ask about ultimate meaning.

In his effort to be faithful to Reformation principles, particularly to the divine transcendence, Barth rejects vehemently the Catholic doctrine of the *analogia entis* as the invention of the antichrist; all other reasons for not becoming Catholic are in his view "shortsighted and lacking in seriousness."[5]

REVELATION

From the Greek *apocalypsis*, "lifting the veil," revelation refers to God's bridging the infinite divide between time and eternity, the Divine and the human, to disclose or communicate something of the Divine Mystery. But God's self-manifestation does not take place in heavenly visions or neatly formulated propositions. We do not encounter God directly; God's revelation or self-disclosure is always mediated by some experience in the world, some person, event, story, or natural phenomenon. The community discerns the divine presence and action through persons, events, and things; expresses it in language and story; and eventually formulates it as religious teaching.

When we review the history of Israel and the earliest Christian communities, it becomes evident that for the peoples of these ancient communities, it was precisely in the events of their ordinary human lives, in encounters both mundane and extraordinary, in tragedy and hope and self-transcendence, in examples of love, compassion, and self-sacrifice, that God's grace became transparent and the divine self-disclosure took place.

In its Dogmatic Constitution on Divine Revelation (*Dei verbum*), the Second Vatican Council taught that God's self-manifestation takes place through God's action in the history of Israel and its interpretation through the words of the prophets and reaches its fullness in the person of God's Son, Jesus the Christ (DV 2–4). Furthermore, the Christian understanding of revelation continues to develop and reach greater depth as the church continues to ponder the mystery from which it lives (DV 9). Thus revelation is not primarily verbal, as Islam teaches, or propositional, as many fundamentalist Christians believe, but personal. From a Christian perspective, revelation means not just that God is the giver of revelation but the gift itself in giving us a share in the divine life as Father, Son, and Holy Spirit (see 2 Pet 1:4).

Similarly, as Edward Schillebeeckx argues, "revelation and experience are not opposites. God's revelation follows the course of human experiences."[6] In this way, a sacred story or myth can be just as much a means of God's self-disclosure as a historical event or prophetic sermon. Thus revelation comes not from outside our world, but from within it, where the transcendent God dwells in an immanent relationship with creation. Revelation is historically mediated. It represents a religious insight or vision emerging from a community of faith "inspired" by the Holy Spirit. For Israel, especially, this revelation emerged from a rereading and retelling of the community's history, while for Christianity it reaches its fullness in the person and history of Jesus of Nazareth and is handed on through the Scripture and Tradition of the church, interpreted by the church's magisterium or teaching office.

FAITH AND REASON

A basic principle of the Catholic tradition is the compatibility of faith and reason, or as it might be expressed today, faith and science.[7] Science and theology are different ways of knowing; they have different methodologies and different understandings of what counts as evidence. Reason cannot arrive on its own at the truths of faith, but neither are those truths contrary to reason, which is not the same as saying that what is true from a theological perspective can be proved scientifically. For example, there is no contradiction between the scientific hypothesis of evolution and the biblical doctrine of creation. One is a scientific description of how the riches of the multitudinous living species developed; the other answers the theological question of what or who is the ultimate cause of life in all its forms.

Both scientists and representatives of religion have erred in claiming exclusive access to truth through their own disciplines. Some scientists have attempted to reduce truth to what can be known through the scientific method of investigation. It is not reason's role to pass judgment on the contents of faith. At the same time, some religious figures have canonized a literalist reading of their sacred texts in the face of clear historical or empirical evidence, for example, to defend a concept of biblical inerrancy that is basically a confessional rather than a biblical position. Fundamentalism is not limited to students of the Bible.

THEOLOGY

From the time of Anselm of Canterbury (d. 1109), theology has been understood as faith seeking understanding (*fides quaerens intellectum*). Theology seeks to bring faith to a deeper understanding; it is a critical reflection on faith, its meaning and implications, sometimes described as the science of faith. In the words of Karl Rahner, theology is "the conscious and methodological explanation and explication of the divine revelation received and grasped in faith."[8] Theology is different from religious studies, which stands outside a tradition to study it critically, while theology presumes a particular faith commitment. It is not primarily an individual effort but the work of the community through whom God's self-disclosure takes place.

Thus, theology has a twofold purpose; one is to hand on faithfully the revelation entrusted to the church, and at the same time, to reflect critically on the church's language, to ensure that it is able to communicate intelligibly to contemporary men and women the riches of what God has revealed. It is a work both of the church and of critical intelligence.

Protestant theology, with its origin in Luther's personal struggle over the question of his righteousness before God, tends to stress the redemption as well as the divine transcendence. In part, the Reformers were influenced by the inheritance of late medieval philosophy, with its univocal concept of being and nominalism, the legacies of Duns Scotus and William of Ockham, respectively.[9] And in part this was a reaction to what the Reformers saw as abuses in Catholic popular devotion and the church's sacramental system. This theological orientation has given a profoundly dialogical character to Protestant theology, a concern to emphasize the difference among the created, the human, and the Divine. Finally, the Reformers were heavily influenced by an Augustinian pessimism. Deeply influenced by Augustine's doctrine of original sin, Calvin described human nature as "totally depraved" (*Institutes* II, 1, 7); the will in bondage, incapable of choosing the good; the intellect blinded, unable to know God apart from grace. God could be known only through Scripture (*sola Scriptura*).

Catholic theology is rooted in the doctrine of the incarnation, the view that in Jesus God has become flesh, entering into space and time and human history. Catholic theology tends to place the emphasis on the divine immanence. It echoes what St. Paul said about God's existence as evident from creation: "For what can be known about God is plain to them" since God's "eternal power and divine nature, invisible though they are, have been understood and seen through the things he has made" (Rom 1:19–20) and grounds what is often referred to as the Catholic sacramental imagination.[10] Its anthropology is more optimistic, seeing nature as damaged but not totally corrupted by original sin.[11]

TRANSCENDENCE AND COMMUNION

If God in Western philosophy and theology is the transcendent Other who is also both immanent and personal, I would like to argue here, following Karl Rahner, that this God as Absolute Being is not far from us. Aside from God's self-revelation in Scripture and the God-man Jesus, the "holy mystery" is both intuited and disclosed, known unthematically or nonconceptually in the experience of transcendence.[12] This transcendental knowledge is an *a posteriori* knowledge, for it is dependent on, or awakened by, our experience of things in the world. But our mind moves always beyond the concrete things that we know to ask the question about where does being itself, that being that "transcends" any particular being, come from?

THE EXPERIENCE OF TRANSCENDENCE

We sense transcendence in the experience of our consciousness moving continually beyond the things that we encounter, to wonder, to question, to dream. We ask why is there anything, where does being come from, when did it begin, and when will it end? Is there life beyond death, intelligence beyond the beauty of the universe, something we sense occasionally on a night filled not with the neon of the cities but the clear white light of the stars? Is there a light beyond the darkness that comes before and after our lives? We have not experienced or sensed these things, yet they are in some way real to us, and we ask about them.

We ask also about truth, are moved by beauty, and sense sometimes the unity of all things, and so we ask: Is there a Truth and Beauty and Oneness that grounds all earthly beings and truth and beauty, what the medieval Scholastics called the transcendentals? We discover in our questioning that we have come face to face with mystery, with Being itself. It is always beyond us, and yet it has touched us and awakened our questions and in some way is disclosed in them. We can think of other examples in which transcendence is disclosed in our self-consciousness, in reflective intelligence.

In the same way, having experienced the love of another, the joy of being known, held, and cherished, we ask about the possibility of a love that lies beyond the loves that are always imperfect and must one day end. Is there an Other who is a Thou, one who holds us in an embrace, who knows our deepest longings and fears, who offers a love that is unending?

Even grasping the finite as finite suggests an experience of transcendence, for if the mind did not transcend the limits of the finite, the finite could not be known as such. The two, the finite and the infinite, are not mutually exclusive; they imply each other. "The finite cannot be known without the Infinite or, to put it differently, the finite is nothing without the Infinite.[13] What this experience of transcendence suggests, with our minds reaching out, our questions moving constantly beyond our limited knowledge, is that we are in some way oriented toward Being itself, not just the things of the world that we know, but Being as such, the mystery that is beyond and in some way grasped, "pre-apprehended," in all our conscious activity.[14] Our knowing takes place against a horizon of Being that is never exhausted by the beings we know.

If we move beyond Rahner's analysis, we will find other philosophers who have made similar observations about what we might call the noetic relationship with Being itself that is disclosed in human consciousness. As Eric Voegelin would say, the very structure of the universe is noetic.[15] The late Robert Neely Bellah spoke of concepts such as God,

Being, Nothingness, and Life as symbols of transcendence that are neither subjective nor objective in their reference. That is, they are based neither on personal, social, or historical experience, nor do they refer to external empirical realities that can be verified in a scientific sense. Rather, they are relational symbols "that are intended to overcome the dichotomies of ordinary conceptualization and bring together the whole of experience," for they don't require a split between ourselves and reality. Reality does not stand "outside" us or over against us; "we participate in reality, not passively but actively."[16]

Similarly, Gordon Kaufman rejects what he calls the mythology of the metaphysical-cosmological dualism found both in the Bible and in Western religious thought, dividing reality into "earth" and "heaven." Even more, this dualism makes it seem as though God were somehow "out there," beyond the realities of our experience.[17] He argues that it is our experience of limit, of finitude or radical contingency, that is the justification for God-language.[18]

Classical theology recognized that the transcendent, ineffable God is beyond all naming, and therefore all our God-language is analogical. Because God is incomprehensible, we are dependent on analogies, metaphors, and symbols to speak meaningfully of God. What is problematic is our tendency to literalize those analogies, metaphors, or symbols, and even more, to canonize those that are masculine.

THE DIVINE OMNIPOTENCE

The notion of God as all powerful is basic to both the Jewish and the Christian understanding of the Divine Mystery, as it is to Scholastic philosophy. Still, this notion of divine omnipotence is a stumbling block for many today who find it difficult to believe in an omnipotent deity when there is so much tragedy and injustice in the world. Why, for example, did God "permit" the holocaust of six million Jews during the Second World War in Europe's dark night under the Nazis? Could God have prevented this slaughter? Is God responsible for tsunamis or earthquakes that kill tens of thousands? Can God change the weather in answer to our prayer? Is God really all powerful?

We need to be careful of our language here, for we are dealing with what ultimately remains mystery. As the creator and author of life, God's power is the cause of the immeasurable universe, the creatures that inhabit it, and the beauty and value that ennoble it. All this God brings into being out of nothing and sustains. Augustine believed that God is always in control, that there is a reason for everything that happens, even if we cannot always discern it, that God's providence will not be frustrated. Yet at the same time, some argue that the divine decision to create a world in which there is genuine spontaneity that reaches its full expression in human freedom means a necessary limitation of the divine omnipotence. If God is to create humans who are able to respond freely in love, God cannot overturn each decision that acts against the divine will for the good of creation.

Therefore, rather than inflating a philosophical notion of the divine omnipotence, it makes more sense to image God mysteriously at work in the world to bring about the divine purpose. The Scholastic notion of God is not the only one possible. For all the limitations of American process philosophy, its authors conceive of God not as unchanging in eternal perfection, as in classical philosophy, but as responsive to the events in the world, even experiencing the world's pain and suffering. Alfred North Whitehead describes God as "the fellow sufferer who understands,"[19] shocking for some of a more traditional mindset, but perhaps not a bad way to understand God. In a similar vein, in his *Spiritual Exercises*, St. Ignatius of Loyola invites the retreatant to consider "how God works and labors for me in all creatures upon the face of the earth."[20]

Today, when more people experience God as absent rather than as present, perhaps we can gain some insight into that mystery of a God whose very "impotence" in the face of our freedom reflects the sovereign creator's love for the creature. In the words of Pope John Paul II, "In a certain sense one could say that confronted with our human freedom, God decided to make Himself 'impotent.'"[21] God's ability to renounce power for persuasion, so unlike our own, is the ultimate witness to God's power, which is really benevolence rather than control. God, who created us as free beings, cannot *not* respect our freedom. In the final analysis, our philosophical and theological efforts to understand God and God's power run head on into the mystery of the divine incomprehensibility. That mystery can be glimpsed but never fully understood. Finally, we are united to God not by our ideas but by love, for God is ultimately personal.

In one of his books, Joseph Ratzinger, later Pope Benedict XVI, roots the possibility of calling on the transcendent God in God's trinitarian nature. He rejects three contemporary arguments against bridging the gap between the transcendent God and the world of finite human beings: first, the rejection of metaphysics itself, and the concept of a creator; second, the modern scientific and technological worldview that rules out any possibility of divine intervention; and finally, the argument that goes back ultimately to Aristotle, that the transcendent by nature cannot enter into relationship with the temporal. He argues that the Christian doctrine of the Trinity reveals that relationship, speech, and logos are present in God.[22] God is not an abstract force or a metaphysical principle, but personal and relational. We can address God because God has already addressed us in Jesus, the Word made flesh.

Perhaps we can gain some insight into this generation of the Word from the Godhead, the only-begotten Son who comes into the world and takes on flesh, from an analogy taken from our own self-consciousness. While consciousness is other directed, becoming its object, our self-consciousness becomes also in a sense other or distinct, beholding ourselves as in a mirror. We experience something analogous to this in dreaming. So also God's self-awareness—infinitely more creative and substantial than ours—becomes a second realization of the Divine Being. Scripture has different metaphors for this.

The Divine Word, or *Logos*, as a personification or perfect expression of God's creative power, is eternally generated (not created) by God the Father. Active in God's creative work, the Logos comes into the world (incarnation) with a mission for God's people. Just as God gives away some of his own being (without loss) in creation, so does God give away himself in the Word, or *Logos*, which becomes a distinct, perfect realization (*hypostasis, persona*) of the Divine Mystery.

The mystery at the heart of the Christian faith that we confess in the Apostles' Creed is the one God who is called Father, Son, and Holy Spirit. This trinitarian language, the result of considerable controversy in the early church, can be easily misunderstood. As we draw this chapter to a close, we need to reflect once more on *what* we are affirming with our God language.

CONCLUSION

In this chapter, we have explored the biblical notion of God. While transcendent, this God is at the same time immanent, Creator of the heavens and the earth and active in history, reaching out to establish a relationship with all men and women. We explored how we can come to know the transcendent God, whether through philosophical reason, revelation, theology, or our own experience of transcendence, and we stressed that in the Catholic tradition, faith and reason are not at odds but complementary. They are different ways of knowing that must work together. We also saw how our different theological anthropologies, Catholic and Protestant, inform the ways we come to know God.

It is this God who leads the children of Israel out of slavery and oppression in Egypt and enters into a covenant relationship with them, chosen to be his own people, a covenant expressed in the Decalogue, especially the first commandment: "I, the Lord, am your God, who brought you out of the land of Egypt, out of the house of slavery; you shall have no other gods before me" (Exod 20:2–3).

Later we must try to express more directly *how* we experience within us this Divine Mystery as Father, Son, and Spirit—this God who shares the divine inner life with us. Now, we turn to how this God, while remaining transcendent, "became flesh and lived among us" (John 1:14) in the person of Jesus of Nazareth.

NOTES

1. Catherine Mowry LaCugna, *God for Us: The Trinity and Christian Life* (San Francisco: HarperSanFrancisco, 1999), 389.

2. Walter Kasper, *Jesus the Christ* (New York: Paulist Press, 1976), 177.

3. Thomas Aquinas, *Summa Theologica*, trans. the Fathers of the English Dominican Province, I,2,3.

4. Robert Barron, *Bridging the Great Divide* (New York: Rowman & Littlefield, 2004), 111.

5. Karl Barth, *Church Dogmatics*, ed. G. W. Bromiley and T. F. Torrance (Edinburgh: T. and T. Clark), I/I *The Doctrine of God* (1936), x.

6. Edward Schillebeeck, *Interim Report on the Books Jesus and Christ* (New York: Crossroad, 1982), 11.

7. See Pope John Paul II's encyclical, *Fides et ratio.*

8. Karl Rahner, "Theology," *Encyclopedia of Theology: The Concise Sacramentum Mundi*, ed. Karl Rahner (New York: Seabury Press, 1975), 1687.

9. See Colin E. Gunton, *The One, the Three, and the Many: God, Creation, and the Culture of Modernity* (Cambridge: Cambridge University Press, 1993), 56–58.

10. See Andrew Greeley, *The Catholic Imagination* (Berkeley: University of California Press, 2000).

11. Thomas P. Rausch, "Catholic Anthropology," in *Teaching the Tradition*, ed. John J. Piderit and Melanie M. Morey (Oxford: Oxford University Press, 2012), 31–45.

12. Karl Rahner, *Foundations of Christian Faith: An Introduction to Christianity* (New York: Seabury Press, 1978), 58.

13. Frederiek Depoortere, *The Death of God: An Investigation into the History of the Western Concept of God* (London: T & T Clark, 2008), 167; see also Anselm K. Min, "Hegel's Absolute: Transcendent or Immanent?" *The Journal of Religion* 56/1 (1976): 68–71.

14. Rahner, *Foundations of Christian Faith*, 33.

15. See Michael P. Morrissey, *Consciousness and Transcendence; The Theology of Eric Voegelin* (Notre Dame, IN: University of Notre Dame Press, 1994), 210.

16. Robert N. Bellah, "Transcendence in Contemporary Piety," in *Transcendence*, ed. Herbert W. Richardson and Donald R. Cutler (Boston: Beacon Press, 1969), 92.

17. Gordon D. Kaufman, "On the Meaning of 'God': Transcendence without Mythology," in Richardson and Cutler, *Transcendence*, 115.

18. Ibid., 120–23.

19. Alfred North Whitehead, *Process and Reality: An Essay in Cosmology* (New York: Free Press, 1978), 351.

20. Ignatius of Loyola, *The Spiritual Exercises of St. Ignatius*, ed. Louis J. Puhl (Chicago: Loyola Press, c. 1951), no. 236.

21. John Paul II, *Crossing the Threshold of Hope*, ed. Vittorio Messori (New York: Random House, 1994), 61.

22. Joseph Ratzinger, *The Feast of Faith* (San Francisco: Ignatius Press, 1986), 18–25.

PART II

Jesus Christ, God's Only Son

CHAPTER 3

THE JESUS
OF THE GOSPELS

While there is little evidence for the life and history of Jesus outside of the New Testament, he appears in the works of two historians from the ancient world, the Jewish Flavius Josephus and the Roman Tacitus. In his *Antiquities of the Jews* (93–94), Josephus touches directly or indirectly on the story of Jesus three times. First, he mentions John the Baptist, "a good man" put to death by Herod (18,5,2). He also refers to James, "the brother of Jesus, who was called Christ," delivered by the Roman procurator Albinus to the Sanhedrin and later stoned (20,9,1). But the most significant reference is to the story of Jesus himself (with two later interpolations by Christian sources identifying him as the Christ and referring to his resurrection). What most scholars judge to be the original version reads as follows:

> At this time there appeared Jesus, a wise man. For he was a doer of startling deeds, a teacher of people who receive the truth with pleasure. And he gained a following among many Jews and among many of Gentile origin. And when Pilate, because of an accusation made by the leading men among us, condemned him to the cross, those who had loved him previously did not cease to do so. And up until this

very day the tribe of Christians (named after him) had not died out. (18,3,3)

Tacitus, a Roman senator as well as a historian, refers in his *Annals* (c. 116) to Jesus' death under Pontius Pilate and to his followers in Rome in the context of the great fire of 64, which Nero blamed on the Christians:

Consequently, to get rid of the report, Nero fastened the guilt and inflicted the most exquisite tortures on a class hated for their abominations, called Christians by the populace. Christus, from whom the name had its origin, suffered the extreme penalty during the reign of Tiberius at the hands of one of our procurators, Pontius Pilatus, and a most mischievous superstition, thus checked for the moment, again broke out not only in Judaea, the first source of the evil, but even in Rome, where all things hideous and shameful from every part of the world find their centre and become popular. Accordingly, an arrest was first made of all who pleaded guilty; then, upon their information, an immense multitude was convicted, not so much of the crime of firing the city, as of hatred against mankind.[1]

There are also two other references. The Roman historian Suetonius (69–122) seems to refer to Jesus' followers as responsible for a disturbance in Rome about 49, though he misspells his name: "Because the Jews at Rome caused continuous disturbances at the instigation of Chrestus [*impulsore Chresto*], he expelled them from the City." Most scholars recognize the passage as a reference to early Christians in Rome.[2] Finally, according to Gerhard Lohfink, the Babylonian Talmud has a reference to Jesus which reads, "[Jesus] practiced magic and led Israel astray" (b. Sotah 47a).[3]

Today, some people, including some scholars, appeal to the apocryphal gospels attributed to figures such as Thomas, Peter, Mary, Magdalene, and Philip for information about Jesus, for example, Dan Brown's sensational *The Da Vinci Code*. However, these pseudo gospels, written considerably later, were not part of the authentic Christian tradition and were never accepted by the church.

Our real information for the story of Jesus comes from the canonical Gospels, Matthew, Mark, Luke, and John. Jesus' ministry began sometime after his baptism at the hands of John the Baptist, and he seems to have spent some time among John's disciples. While John warned of God's coming judgment, Jesus' own religious experience was different, more positive. Ultimately, he left John's company and began to gather his own disciples.

The Gospels present Jesus as proclaiming the good news (*euangelion*) that the kingdom of God was at hand. He healed the sick, reached out to the troubled and the marginal, proclaimed that sins were forgiven and the poor blessed. He sought to reconstitute Israel as the community of salvation, building his movement around "the twelve" (Mark 3:13–19), symbolic of the original twelve tribes and teaching his disciples to minister as he did (Mark 6:12–13; Matt 10:5–8). But his preaching and ministry occasioned opposition from both the Jewish and the occupying Roman authorities, and he was put to death—crucified, the humiliating capital punishment reserved by the Romans for revolutionaries and others who challenged the authority of imperial Rome.

DEVELOPMENT OF THE GOSPEL TRADITION

The gospel tradition developed in the early churches over a period of some seventy years. The first Gospel was Mark, traditionally dated to the year 68, while the last was John, which appeared close to the end of the first century (95). The first three Gospels, Mark, Matthew, and Luke, are referred to as the Synoptics (from the Greek *synoptikos*, seen together), since Matthew and Luke are largely dependent on Mark, though each had their own sources and both make use of a collection of the sayings of Jesus unknown to Mark, called Q, from the German *Quelle*. From Q come important elements of the Jesus tradition, including the Lord's Prayer and the Beatitudes.

While there is considerable historical information contained in the Gospels, it would be a mistake to consider them as histories in our modern sense; the gospel writers are evangelists or preachers and sometimes shape the material in light of their own insights and the needs of their churches. An important document of the Vatican's Pontifical Biblical Commission, *Instruction on the Historical Truth of the Gospels* (1964), stressed that the gospels are not literal, chronological reports of the words and deeds of the historical Jesus but are the products of a tradition that goes through three distinct stages: the original words and deeds of the Jesus of history, the oral preaching of the early Christian churches, and the actual writing of the Gospels by the evangelists. Two important recent works in Christology stress that the Jesus of the Gospels is the Jesus of history, even if they recognize this process of development.[4]

We could summarize the three stages in the development of the gospel tradition as follows:

First Stage: Words and deeds of the Jesus of history: actual words, phrases, expressions, of the Jesus of history; what he taught, what he did, what happened to him. Some examples would include his sayings, his parables, and his use of "Abba" in prayer.

Second Stage: Oral preaching of the early Christian communities. This material was circulating in the community for more than thirty years before the first Gospel, Mark, was composed. It included:

Easter kerygma = proclamation of the resurrection of Jesus (1 Cor 15:3–8; AA 2:32–36)

Sayings of Jesus = Q source (Beatitudes, Our Father, Sabbath sayings, sayings about marriage and divorce)

Collections of parables

Stories about Jesus (baptism, table fellowship, passion, and others)

Miracle stories

Catechetical material

Hymns (Phil 2:6–11; John 1:1–16; Luke 1:46–55, 68–79)

Liturgical formulas (Mark 8:6; Matt 28:19)

Doxologies (2 Cor 13:14)

Christological titles (prophet, Son of David, messiah, Lord, Son of Man, Son of God, Emmanuel, God)

Easter stories (discovery of empty tomb, appearance stories)

Third Stage: Actual writing by the evangelists: Matthew, Mark, Luke, John

What this research shows is that there was a great deal of what we might call "Jesus material" circulating in the early Christian communities or churches long before there were any written gospels; these churches were preaching the gospel, telling the stories of what Jesus did and said, giving witness to his resurrection, collecting his parables and the stories of his miracles, preparing candidates for baptism, celebrating the Eucharist or Lord's Supper, using hymns and doxologies in their worship, and reflecting on ministry in relation to the example of Jesus. In other words, the Gospels come from the church, not the church from the Gospels.

HEARING THE VOICE OF JESUS

We can hear the voice of Jesus especially in his sayings and parables. While both have sometimes been refined or added to by the evangelists in writing to their communities, careful scholarship can recognize what comes from Jesus himself in the sayings and parables as they have been handed down to us.

SAYINGS OF JESUS

While there are many sayings preserved in the gospels, many of them come from the Q source. Especially important are the Beatitudes. Notice that Matthew and Luke have slightly different versions, and Luke adds some "woes." While both versions have been adapted to include the disciples and others, they contain sayings addressed to the poor, the hungry, and those who mourn, and thus reflect the emphasis on God's special concern for the poor and the powerless so evident in the prophetic tradition.

According to Daniel Harrington, the Beatitudes "offer a sketch of character traits, attitudes and virtues that are fitting for those seeking the kingdom of God."[5] The great

Matthew 5:3–12

Blessed are the poor in spirit, for theirs is the kingdom of heaven.

Blessed are they who mourn, for they will be comforted.

[Blessed are the meek, for they will inherit the land.]

Blessed are they who hunger and thirst for righteousness, for they will be satisfied.

[Blessed are the merciful, for they will be shown mercy.

Blessed are the clean of heart, for they will see God.

Blessed are the peacemakers, for they will be called children of God.

Blessed are they who are persecuted for the sake of righteousness, for theirs is the kingdom of heaven.]

Blessed are you when they insult you and persecute you and utter every kind of evil against you [falsely] because of me.

Rejoice and be glad, for your reward will be great in heaven. Thus they persecuted the prophets who were before you.

Luke 6:20–26

Blessed are you who are poor, for the kingdom of God is yours.

Blessed are you who are now hungry, for you will be satisfied.

Blessed are you who are now weeping, for you will laugh.

Blessed are you when people hate you, and when they exclude you and insult you, and denounce your name as evil on account of the Son of Man.

Rejoice and leap for joy on that day! Behold, your reward will be great in heaven. For their ancestors treated the prophets in the same way.

[But woe to you who are rich, for you have received your consolation.

But woe to you who are filled now, for you will be hungry.

Woe to you who laugh now, for you will grieve and weep.

Woe to you when all speak well of you, for their ancestors treated the false prophets in this way.]

eschatological sermon in Mathew 25:31–46 is in the same tradition.

In addition to the Beatitudes, we will consider here fifteen sayings of Jesus, selected by the great Lutheran scholar Rudolf Bultmann and accepted by most scholars as authentic.[6]

1. "If a kingdom is divided against itself, that kingdom cannot stand. And if a house is divided against itself, that house will not be able to stand. And if Satan has risen up against himself and is divided, he cannot stand, but his end has come" (Mark 3:24–26).

2. "But no one can enter a strong man's house and plunder his property without first tying up the strong man; then indeed the house can be plundered" (Mark 3:27).

3. "For whoever wishes to save his life will lose it, but whoever loses his life for my sake and that of the gospel will save it" (Mark 8:35).

4. "No one who sets a hand to the plow and looks back is fit for the kingdom of God" (Luke 9:62).

5. "How hard it will be for those who have wealth to enter the kingdom of God" (Mark 10:23b).

6. "It is easier for a camel to go through the eye of a needle than for someone who is rich to enter the kingdom of God" (Mark 10:25).

7. "Let the dead bury their own dead" (Luke 9:60a).

8. "Enter through the narrow gate; for the gate is wide and the road is easy that leads to destruction, and there are many who take it. For the gate is narrow and the road is hard that leads to life, and there are few who find it" (Matt 7:13–14).

9. "But many who are first will be last, and the last will be first" (Mark 10:31).

10. "There is nothing outside a person that by going in can defile, but the things that come out are what defile" (Mark 7:15).

11. "Truly I tell you, whoever does not receive the kingdom of God as a little child will never enter it" (Mark 10:15).

12. "For all who exalt themselves will be humbled, and those who humble themselves will be exalted" (Luke 14:11).

13. "You are those who justify yourselves in the sight of others; but God knows your hearts; for what is prized by human beings is an abomination in the sight of God" (Luke 16:15).

14. "But if anyone strikes you on the right cheek, turn the other also; and if anyone wants to sue you and take your coat, give your cloak as well; and if anyone forces you to go one mile, go also the second mile" (Matt 5:39b–41).

15. "Love your enemies and pray for those who persecute you, so that you may be children of your Father in heaven; for he makes his sun rise on the evil and on the good, and sends rain on the righteous and on the unrighteous. For if you love those who love you, what reward do you have? Do not even the tax collectors do the same? And if you greet only your brothers and sisters, what more are you doing than others? Do not even the Gentiles do the same? Be perfect, therefore, as your heavenly Father is perfect" (Matt 5:44–48).

There are certainly other sayings of Jesus contained in the Gospels; some are embedded in stories about Jesus or in his parables, and others were occasioned by his healings. But these are certainly authentic and reflect themes characteristic of the preaching of Jesus. We note the following: the centrality of the kingdom of God (4, 5, 6, 11), a final reversal of status (3, 6, 9, 12), struggle or conflict (1, 2, 3, 4, 8), the danger of wealth (5, 6), and the call for a radical change of heart (4, 10, 11, 14, 15).

Too often Christians have a tendency to overlook or avoid the more challenging sayings of Jesus, those about changing one's life, concern for the poor, and judgment. We want to "domesticate" Jesus, make his teachings more acceptable. But there was something intrinsically challenging about his preaching. In these sayings we capture again his voice. His language is disturbing, unsettling, calling us to a radical conversion, a different way of life, a different outlook, what the Gospels call *metanoia*, Greek for a total change of heart, mind, consciousness, and outlook.

THE PARABLES

Even more disturbing are the parables. Consider, for example, the parable of the workers in the vineyard (Matt 20:1–16). When we hear it, many of us think it terribly unfair; those who worked the whole day in the heat of the sun receive the same wages as those who were hired at the last hour of the day. Why should they get the same? Isn't that unjust? Shouldn't those who worked all day receive more? But the parable describes the incredible generosity of God. Even more, it shows God's special concern for the poor, the desperate, those who had no work to enable them to feed their families, because "no one hired us."

Parables are stories that combine metaphor with narrative. Taken from the everyday world of nature and ordinary human activity, they are about laborers and fishermen, farmers and merchants, landlords and those in debt; they tell sto-

The Jesus of the Gospels

ries of wedding feasts, travelers, seeds, harvests, and bread baking. Some have multiple meanings, or we find ourselves identifying with unexpected characters in the story, like the unforgiving older brother in the parable of the prodigal son.

The parables challenge our ordinary way of thinking, open up new perspectives, disturb us, and force us to examine our values. Consider the good Samaritan (Luke 10:29–37), the rich man and Lazarus (Luke 16:19–35), the marriage feast (Matt 22:1–14), the parable of the talents (Matt 25:14–30), the sheep and the goats (Matt 25:31–46). Others such as the lost sheep, the lost coin (Luke 15:1–10), and the prodigal son (Luke 15:11–32) suggest a new way of imagining God. Eamonn Bredin points out that there is something shocking and subversive about the parables of Jesus: "It is the *Samaritan* who is neighbor, it is the *last* who are first, it is the *lost* who are rejoiced over, the *stranger* who is at table, the *wastrel* son who is embraced and fêted."[7] When we meditate on the parables, we gain an insight into the kingdom of God breaking into our world.

THE KINGDOM OF GOD

At the very center of the preaching of Jesus is the metaphor of the kingdom of God. Though he does not define it, as a teacher would do in a classroom, the kingdom is the object of many of his sayings and parables. The kingdom of God is like a farmer sowing seed in his field, a grain of mustard seed planted in the earth, a woman mixing leaven in the dough, or a merchant searching for fine pearls (Matt 13).

The roots of the kingdom of God in Jesus' preaching are to be found in the Old Testament image of Yahweh as king. In the ancient world, kings had absolute power, the power of life or death, so kingship was a fitting metaphor for God. Even prior to the establishment of the monarchy, Yahweh was understood as king of Israel (Deut 33:5; 1 Sam 8:7). Later the biblical authors extended God's reign far beyond Israel. Thus, in the Psalms Yahweh appears as the God who reigns over Israel (Ps 95), over other nations (Pss 22:29; 47; 99), and finally, as a cosmic king ruling over all creation in virtue of his work as creator (Pss 74:12; 93; 95—99).

In some of the later prophetic writings, Yahweh's reign takes on a messianic, eschatological perspective; the prophets look forward to the final establishment of Yahweh's reign when God's salvation would appear in its fullness (Obad 21; Zeph 3:15–20; Zech 14:16–21). The notion of God's reign is a frequent theme in the late Old Testament and in some of the noncanonical, inter-testamental writings, where the reign of God is associated with apocalyptic displays of God's power and judgment and the establishment of Israel's rule over the nations. N. T. Wright argues that within Second Temple Judaism, the theme of God's kingdom evoked a "complete story-line" that envisioned Israel's final return from exile, a correlative return of Yahweh to Zion, as well as Yahweh's victory over evil in the form of Israel's enemies.[8]

The kingdom of God is at the heart of Jesus' message and is well attested in the gospel tradition, appearing over 150 times. It is present in the Q tradition, in Mark, in the material unique to Matthew and to Luke, in John, and throughout the Pauline corpus. It is the center of Jesus' Sermon on the Mount and the subject of most of his parables. The kingdom functions as a polyvalent symbol; as Eamonn Bredin notes, it is "approaching," "coming," "at hand" (Mark 1:15; Matt 10:7; Luke 10:11). One is called to "enter into" (Mark 9:47; 10:23–25; Matt 5:20; 18:3; John 3:5) or "seek" it (Matt 6:33; Luke 12:31). Some are "not far" from it (Mark 12:34). Others fail to enter it (Mark 10:15; Matt 7:21). The kingdom is a secret not revealed to everyone (Mark 4:11); there are "keys" to it given to some (Matt 16:19). Most of all, it "has come upon you" (Matt 12:28; Luke 11:20) or "is in the midst of you" (Luke 17:21).[9]

Thus, the idea of the kingdom of God was familiar to those who listened to Jesus. Some of them, like the Zealots, interpreted it in terms of freedom from Roman rule and were not adverse to the use of violence to realize their goal. For this reason Jesus was cautious about accepting the title *messiah*, lest his message be interpreted as a call to revolution. When asking the disciples about who people say that he is, Peter answers, "You are the Christ." Jesus tells them not to tell anyone about him (Mark 8:29–30).

CHARACTERISTICS OF THE KINGDOM

First of all, the kingdom of God is a dynamic concept in Jesus' preaching. While the Greek of the Gospels uses the word *basileia*, "kingdom," it is better translated as "reign" or "rule." The kingdom refers not to a place but to a dynamic event, God exercising his saving power or reign among people in a new way through the ministry of Jesus. I will use both expressions here. It means that Israel's hope for salvation has arrived.

Kenan Osborne offers the following phrases as "substitutes" for the symbol of the kingdom of God:[10]

Presence of God	Justice of God
Love of God	Holiness of God
Compassion of God	Goodness of God
Mercy of God	Creativeness of God
Power of God	Grace of God
Forgiveness of God	Relatedness of God

THE KINGDOM AS PRESENT

There is also an eschatological tension in Jesus' preaching of the kingdom; it is present *and* future, realized and still to come in its fullness. The reign of God is present in his preaching and his parables, his miracles and exorcisms, his practice of table fellowship, and his proclamation of the forgiveness of sins.

PREACHING AND PARABLES

Both the sayings of Jesus (Mark 1:15) and the parables show that the kingdom of God is near at hand or present. The seed that falls on the rocky ground (Matt 3—8), the wheat growing slowly with the weeds (24—30), the tiny mustard seed that becomes the large bush (31—32), the yeast mixed in with the flour (33), the treasure buried in the field (44), the pearl of great price (45—46), or the net thrown into the sea (47—50) all show that the reign of God is already present, growing, transforming, and gathering. Jesus' departure from John the Baptist's movement was at least in part over this issue of the presence of the reign of God.

MIRACLES AND EXORCISMS

Jews at the time of Jesus saw sickness or infirmity as the work of demonic power (Luke 13:10–16) or the result of sin (John 9:1–3). Jesus' exorcisms (Mark 1:23–28; 3:23–27) and his healings show that God's salvific power was becoming effective in the broken bodies and damaged spirits of the people to whom he ministered, healing them and setting them free. Driving out demons or evil spirits does not need to be interpreted literally as demonic possession. In this prescientific society, psychological and medical phenomena such as epilepsy, psychotic breakdowns, or controlling addictions were ascribed to evil spirits. They prevented people from being free, just as they do today. Jesus' exorcisms show that the power of evil was being broken. When he was charged with driving out demons by the power of Beelzebul, he responded, "But if it is by the finger of God that I cast out the demons, then the kingdom of God has come to you" (Luke 11:20). The saying is almost certainly authentic.

THE FORGIVENESS OF SIN

Jesus' proclamation of the forgiveness of sins scandalized some of the scribes and Pharisees, who objected, "Who can forgive sins but God alone?" (Mark 2:7). But forgiveness was an important part of Jesus' ministry. It meant reconciliation with God and with the community. It was more evidence that the age of salvation was at hand. As N. T. Wright points out, instead of situating the blessings of salvation in Temple and Torah, Jesus was claiming that they were available now for those who trusted in him and in the kingdom he proclaimed. He was replacing adherence to Temple and Torah with allegiance to himself.[11] Whether or not he actually said "your sins are forgiven" in so many words, he proclaimed forgiveness, not only in words and parables (Matt 18:23–35; Luke 15:11–32), but also in deeds. Here, especially, the table fellowship tradition is important, as we will see below.

TABLE FELLOWSHIP

To share a meal with someone in the Middle East, even today, is a sign of communion. In Jesus' time, to share bread at table over which the head of the house had asked a blessing signified fellowship with God, while the purity laws forbade associating with those who were unclean or outside the Law. They were marginalized from the community. The distinctions between the clean and the unclean as well as between sinners and the righteous found concrete expression in the rules governing table fellowship,[12] and righteous Jews were expected to observe these rules.

Yet much of Jesus' ministry took place at meals, meals shared with his disciples, in the houses of some of the leading figures in the community like Simon the Pharisee (Luke 7:36), with the multitude that followed him, as in the story of the miracle of the loaves, and with the religiously marginalized, those stigmatized in the Gospels as "tax collectors and sinners" (Mark 2:15; Matt 11:19). Jesus relativized the purity laws by teaching that "nothing outside a person that by going in can defile, but the things that come out are what defile" (Mark 7:15).

And while conversion of life and outlook was an important part of his preaching, his table fellowship and the criticism it occasioned shows that no one was excluded from God's reign. In this way he proclaimed the forgiveness of sin in deeds. Meyer points out that Jesus' openness to sinners did not mean that he acquiesced in their sins. But he reversed the normal pattern, first conversion, and then communion. His offer of communion with sinners triggered repentance; thus "conversion flowered from communion."[13]

THE KINGDOM AS STILL TO COME

At the same time, there is clearly a future dimension to the Jesus preaching of God's reign, a kingdom yet to come. In the Lord's Prayer, he teaches his disciples to pray, "Thy kingdom come" (Matt 6:9; Luke 11:2). The sayings about the Son of Man coming in judgment emphasize the future dimension of God's reign (Mark 14:62; Matt 25:31–32; 26:64; Luke 12:8–9). The parables of the kingdom—the farmer and the seed, the weeds and the wheat, the mustard seed, the yeast kneaded in the flour, the net cast into the sea (Matt 13:1–53)—bring both the present and future aspects of God's reign to light.

Gerhard Lohfink stresses the eschatological notion of the "gathering" of the scattered people of God, a frequent theme in postexilic theology. The concept, always God's work (see Deut 30:1–5; Isa 11:12–13; 56:8; Ps 147:2–3), is parallel to the notion of "liberating," "saving," "healing," and "redeeming" Israel. This gathering theme appears frequently in Jesus' ministry, but here it is dependent on a decision for or against himself (Matt 12:30; Luke 11:23), reflective of his desire to gather the children of Jerusalem as a hen gathers her brood (Matt 23:37; Luke 13:34). It appears again though in a different form in the petition "hallowed be thy name" in the Lord's Prayer (Matt 6:9; Luke 11:2), echoing Ezekiel 36:19–28, where Yahweh makes holy his name in gathering Israel from among the nations, and it is symbolized in Jesus' choice of "the twelve" as the foundation for the eschatological people of God.[14]

The full meaning of God's reign would not be understood until after the resurrection. But the tension between present and future realization is still present in John's Gospel, though John substitutes "eternal life" for the metaphor of the kingdom. "Those who eat my flesh and drink my blood have eternal life, and I will raise them up on the last day" (6:54).

CONTEMPORARY EXPRESSIONS OF THE KINGDOM OF GOD

In every age the church must translate Jesus' preaching of the nearness or presence of the kingdom of God into contemporary language. Some put the emphasis on God's activity in the midst of our world and in our lives. Others stress how God's saving grace is mediated to others through love and compassionate service, while still others describe it from the perspective of liberation theology.

Michael Cook sees "kingdom of God" as Jesus' comprehensive term for the blessings of salvation insofar as it denotes the divine activity at the center of human life, while "faith" is Jesus' human, existential term for salvation insofar as it denotes the human response of openness, acceptance, and commitment to his preaching.[15] Edward Schillebeeckx, a Flemish Dominican, contrasts John the Baptist's warning of a coming judgment with Jesus' message of hope; the good news he proclaimed was of God's action now present within human history and in our own human lives and mediated or made visible by human beings caring for one another.[16]

Albert Nolan, another Dominican involved in the struggle against apartheid in South Africa, described the kingdom of God as a kingdom of love and service that reveals God as a God of compassion. For it is precisely human compassion that "releases God's power in the world, the only power that can bring about the miracle of the kingdom."[17] Jon Sobrino, one of the Jesuits of El Salvador, who escaped murder—the fate of the other members of his community carried out by Salvadoran military forces in 1989—while he was in Thailand, writes about the kingdom of God from the perspective of liberation theology. He describes Jesus as calling others to a radical discipleship that would place them at the disposal of the kingdom. He borrows an image from Ignatio

Ellacuría, killed with the others that night, challenging those who would be disciples at the service of the kingdom to take the crucified peoples of the world down from the cross.

Feminist theologian Elisabeth Schüssler Fiorenza argues that the reign of God is being realized wherever people are being healed, set free from oppression or dehumanizing power systems, and made whole.[18] Terrence Tilley describes the reign of God as a realm of human flourishing. Like those in the Jesus' Movement, Christians continuing the practices of the reign of God: healing, exorcising, sharing table fellowship, forgiving, and teaching, and they do this not just as individuals but by working to transform society.[19]

Pope Benedict XVI, who fears that liberation theologies end up making the kingdom the work of human beings rather than of God, says that "the new proximity of the Kingdom of which Jesus speaks...is to be found in Jesus himself. Through Jesus' presence and action, God has here and now entered actively into history in a wholly new way. The reason why *now* is the fullness of time (Mk 1:15), why *now* is in a unique sense the time of conversion and penance, as well as the time of joy, is that in Jesus it is God who draws near to us."[20]

Finally, we might quote St. Paul, who says simply that "the kingdom of God is not food and drink but righteousness and peace and joy in the Holy Spirit" (Rom 14:17).

CONCLUSION

While there are a few extra-biblical references to Jesus of Nazareth, most of our information about his life and ministry comes from the Gospels. We hear his voice particularly in his sayings and parables and in his preaching on the kingdom of God. Jesus challenged the values of this world; he called the people to a radical change of heart, warned about the danger of riches, and called blessed the poor, the hungry, the merciful, and peacemakers.

The kingdom or reign of God was a metaphor of God's saving power breaking into the lives of men and women through the ministry of Jesus, healing the sick, setting free those under the power of evil, reconciling sinners and those marginalized from the religious community, and gathering together a community of salvation. Ultimately, his preaching and efforts to symbolize a renewed Israel, with the Twelve at its center, aroused strong opposition on the part of the Jewish authorities in Jerusalem. With the help of the Roman governor, he was condemned and put to death on a cross, a Roman form of capital punishment reserved for slaves and those who rebelled against Rome.

Contemporary theology sees God's reign as being mediated or realized through the compassionate service of others, in works of reconciliation, care for the poor, and freeing the disadvantaged from oppressive structures. But the kingdom of God cannot be reduced to an ideology or program for social change; it is inseparable from God drawing near to us through the life and teaching of Jesus, God's only Son.

NOTES

1. Tacitus, *Annals* 15.44, in *Documents and Images for the Study of Paul*, ed. Neil Elliott and Mark Reasoner, trans. Church and Brodribb (Minneapolis, MN: Fortress Press, 2010), 58.

2. N. T. Wright, *The New Testament and the People of God* (Minneapolis: Fortress Press, 1992), 354–55; Suetonius, *Lives of the Caesars: Claudius* (London: Loeb Classical Library, 1914), 25.4; cf. Acts 18:2.

3. Gerhard Lohfink, *Jesus of Nazareth: What He Wanted, Who He Was* (Collegeville, MN: Liturgical Press, 2012), 274.

4. Pope Benedict XVI, *Jesus of Nazareth*, part 1 (New York:

Doubleday, 2007) and *Jesus of Nazareth, Part Two* (San Francisco: Ignatius Press, 2011); Lohfink, *Jesus of Nazareth*.

5. Daniel J. Harrington, *Jesus: A Historical Portrait* (Cincinnati, OH: St. Anthony Messenger Press, 2007), 33.

6. Rudolf Bultmann, *The History of the Synoptic Tradition* (Oxford: Basil Blackwell, 1963), 102–4.

7. Eamonn Bredin, *Rediscovering Jesus: Challenge of Discipleship* (Quezon City, Philippines: Claretian Publications, 1986), 43.

8. N. T. Wright, *Jesus and the Victory of God* (Minneapolis: Fortress, 1996), 204–7.

9. Bredin, *Rediscovering Jesus*, 25.

10. Kenan B. Osborne, *The Resurrection of Jesus: New Considerations for Its Theological Interpretation* (New York: Paulist, 1997), 150.

11. Cf. Wright, *Jesus and the Victory of God*, 274.

12. Ben F. Meyer, *The Aims of Jesus* (London: SCM Press, 1979), 159.

13. Ibid., 161.

14. Lohfink, *Jesus of Nazareth*, 59–71.

15. Michael Cook, *The Jesus of Faith: A Study in Christology* (New York: Paulist Press, 1981), 56–57.

16. Edward Schillebeeckx, *Jesus: An Experiment in Christology* (New York: Seabury, 1979).

17. Albert Nolan, *Jesus before Christianity* (Maryknoll, NY: Orbis Books, 1978), 84.

18. Elisabeth Schüssler Fiorenza, *In Memory of Her: A Feminist Reconstruction of Christian Origins* (New York: Crossroad, 1994), 123.

19. Terrence Tilley, *The Disciples Jesus: Christology as Reconciling Practice* (Maryknoll, NY: Orbis Books, 2008).

20. Pope Benedict XVI, *Jesus of Nazareth*, 1:60–61.

CHAPTER 4

CHRISTOLOGY

With the cross or crucifix—icons of Christian faith—so common, it is difficult for us to appreciate the devastating effect the death of Jesus had on the disciples. Fearful of suffering a similar fate, they fled Jerusalem (except for the women), returning to Galilee, their hopes shattered. As the two disciples on the road to Emmaus put it, "We had hoped that he was the one to redeem Israel" (Luke 24:21).

And yet, within a short time, these men and women became convinced that Jesus was alive; they spoke of him as exalted to God's right hand, that he had been raised from the dead, that he was still in their midst. The resurrection is at the very heart of the New Testament; without it nothing holds together, and the Jesus' Movement would have died, like so many others lost to history. In this chapter we consider the foundations of the church's Christology, including the death of Jesus, the mystery of his resurrection, christological titles, and the church's interpretation of his story.

THE DEATH OF JESUS

Clearly, Jesus challenged the authority of the religious leaders of the Jewish community of his day. His willingness to interpret the Torah or Law in his preaching and his extending God's love to the religiously marginal, the "tax collectors and sinners," represented a clear claim to an authority of his own. But their opposition to Jesus must have been based on something more.

Mark reports a number of accusations against Jesus at the hearing before the Sanhedrin. He was quoted as saying, "I will destroy this temple that is made with hands, and in three days I will build another, not made with hands" (Mark 14:58). The high priest accused him of blasphemy for claiming to be "the Messiah, the Son of the Blessed One" (Mark 14:61). Others mocked him, saying, "Prophesy" (Mark 14:65), implying that he claimed to be a prophet. At his trial before the Roman procurator, Pilate asked him, "Are you the king of the Jews?" and the soldiers mocked him, using this title. The charge of having messianic pretensions certainly would have been a serious offense for the Roman governor. What was the offense that lay behind the death of Jesus?

A good number of scholars see the so-called cleansing of the Temple as the provocation that led to the execution of Jesus.[1] Too often this story, told in all four Gospels, is interpreted as a story of outraged piety; Jesus drives out the moneychangers and those who sold small birds and other animals in the Temple precincts. But his action was considerably more. It was a prophetic sign on the part of Jesus, symbolizing the Temple's destruction. Mark brackets his account of this incident in the Temple with the story of Jesus cursing a barren fig tree, the only negative miracle in the Gospels (Mark 11:11–21). In Mark and Matthew, the onlookers at the crucifixion repeat the charge that Jesus would destroy and rebuild the Temple (Mark 15:29; Matt 27:40). And John's version of the incident includes a saying about destruction and rebuilding (John 2:19).

The sellers and moneychangers were necessary for the Temple cult, which was based on animal sacrifice. In driving them out, Jesus was striking at the Temple's heart, closing down its cult, at least temporarily; he was saying that its time was over, for Israel had not recognized his coming. He was saying that both Temple and nation would soon be destroyed, as indeed they were. This was too much for the high priests, and they conspired with the Roman procurator to have Jesus executed, crucified.

Reserved for slaves, pirates, and enemies of the Roman state, crucifixion was a cruel method of putting a condemned person to a slow and humiliating death. Victims were often scourged first, then stripped naked, fastened to a cross with rope or nails, and left to die in full public view. Sometimes their legs were broken to hasten death. It has been said that six thousand followers of Spartacus were crucified along the Appian Way in 71 BCE after his failed slave rebellion, while Josephus reports that the Romans crucified people along the walls of Jerusalem. The disciples of Jesus were shattered by his crucifixion, apparently returning to Galilee.

THE MYSTERY OF THE RESURRECTION

Yet within a relatively short period of time, the disciples were proclaiming that God had exalted Jesus to his right hand (Acts 2:35; 5:31), that he had been taken into heaven (Luke 24:51; Acts 1:11), that God had raised him from the dead. The New Testament uses these different images to confess that the Crucified One lived. Still, what is often referred to as the disciples' Easter experience remains something of a mystery. It is not possible to say exactly what they experienced, except that they were convinced that God had vindicated Jesus, that he was alive, with God, and with them.

What prepared the disciples to recognize the risen Jesus? In Greek thought, the human person was conceived dualistically; the human person was a composite of body and spirit, or as some of the Platonists taught, a soul that was capable of surviving the death of the body. But in most of the Hebrew Scriptures, there is no idea of life beyond the grave. A person who died went down into Sheol, really a synonym for death or the grave. Sheol was a place of darkness, a shadow land with no life or activity. Worst of all, in Sheol there was no relationship with Yahweh (Ps 88:7, 13), no praise of his name (Pss 6:6; 115:17), though as Joseph Ratzinger notes, occasionally the alternative tradition surfaced in the literature that communion with God could not be ended even by death (Ps 73:22–28).[2]

It was only very late during the persecution of the Jews under Antioch IV (167–64 BCE), when Jews were being put to death for the practice of their faith, that they began to ask what it meant to die in faithfulness to Yahweh. Could the God who created the heavens and the earth also give life to the dead? It was at this time that the idea of the resurrection of the dead entered into the Jewish imagination (Dan 12:1–3; 2 Macc 7:9, 14, 23; 12:44–45; 14:46). But two comments here: First, the idea was of a general resurrection of the dead that would accompany God's apocalyptic breaking into history, which may be one of the reasons many of the disciples associated the resurrection of Jesus with his immanent *parouisa* or second coming. Second, the Jewish community at the time of Jesus was divided on the subject of the resurrection; some, like the Pharisees, believed in it, while the more conservative Sadducees, who accepted only the Torah (the Law, represented by the first five books of the Jewish Scriptures), did not, as we know from the dilemma posed by the Sadducees to Jesus about the woman with the seven husbands (cf. Luke 20:27–38; Acts 23:1–8).

THE EASTER TRADITION

The Easter tradition in the New Testament appears in two different forms. First, there is the Easter kerygma or proclamation, that is short, formulaic statements of belief that God has raised Jesus from the dead and that there are witnesses (Luke 24:34; Acts 2:32; 3:15; 5:31; 10:40; Rom 10:9). One of the oldest, pre-Pauline, appears in 1 Cor 15:3–7:

> For I handed on to you as of first importance what I in turn had received: that Christ died for our sins in accordance with the scriptures, and that he was buried, and that he was raised on the third day in accordance with the scriptures, and that he appeared to Cephas, then to the twelve. Then he appeared to more than five hundred brothers and sisters at one time, most of whom are still alive, though some have died. Then he appeared to James, then to all the apostles.

By contrast, the Easter stories are later, more expansive, dramatic narratives. They include the discovery of the empty tomb in Jerusalem and the appearances of Jesus to the disciples, probably first in Galilee. The stories are later. Notice that Mark has the story of the discovery of the empty tomb, the basis of which is probably historical, but no appearance stories, if one excludes the later Markan appendices or endings, obviously dependent on the later Gospels.

THE DISCIPLES' EASTER EXPERIENCE

The appearance stories represent not so much historical accounts of the disciples' experience but theological stories to help others to come to Easter faith. Thus, they teach that the risen Jesus is to be encountered in "the breaking of the bread" or Eucharist (Luke 24:31, 35); that the disciples have authority to teach, baptize, and forgive sins (Matt 28:19–20; John 20:23); that one does not have to see to be a believer (John 20:29); and that Peter has pastoral authority over the flock (John 21:15–17). According to Gerhard Lohfink, the "inner structure" of the disciples' Easter experience can be regarded as genuine appearances of the Risen One, "in which God revealed his Son in power and in all his glory (Gal 1:16) but *psychologically* at the same time as visions in which the disciples' power of imagination constructed the appearance of the Risen One."[3]

If there remains a certain element of mystery about the Easter experience of the disciples, there are some conclusions we can draw. First of all, it is important to walk a fine line between seeing the resurrection as itself an object of faith, that is to say, something created by the disciples as they reflected on their experience of Jesus, and seeing it as an objective event open to any observer. To describe it as an object of faith would be to make it an entirely subjective event, as some theologians still under the influence of the post-Enlightenment rationalism would argue.

At that same time, some theologians argue that the resurrection was not a historical event, not in the sense that it wasn't real, but meaning that it cannot be proved. No one observed the resurrection itself; there could not have been "film at eleven"! What counts as evidence is not the actual resurrection but the testimony of the witnesses, the empty tomb, and Christianity itself. The resurrection was real in that it happened not in the imagination of the disciples, but to Jesus. As an act of God upon Jesus, the resurrection should be considered as an eschatological event, a trans-historical event that lies outside the conditions of space and time, but one that has left its traces on history.

Second, notice that Jesus appeared, not to his enemies, to

those whose hearts were closed to him, but to the disciples, to those who loved him and had opened to him their hearts and their lives. He did not appear to the high priest Annas, to the Sanhedrin, or to Pontius Pilate, whose hearts were closed to him. The resurrection appearances do not compel faith, for God always respects our freedom. In the appearance stories, the disciples react with fear, nonrecognition, and disbelief; they think they are seeing a ghost. Even Mary Magdalene, who loved Jesus, mistakes him for the gardener (John 20:15). There is something nonobjectifiable about these stories. What are they trying to tell us?

One has the impression that Jesus has to lead the disciples to Easter faith, inviting them to touch him and eating in their presence (Luke 24:39, 41–42) or showing them his wounded hands and side (John 20:27; cf. Luke 24:40). Some continued to doubt even when he appeared to them (Matt 28:17). In other words, while the Easter experience of the disciples was unique, it was more similar to ours than different. The only exception might be the case of Paul, but Paul, however misguided, was a sincere searcher, a deeply religious man open to the revelation he ultimately received (Gal 1:16). It changed the life of this rigid Pharisee into a zealous apostle, and he remained forever grateful, talking in his writings about the glorious freedom of the children of God (Rom 8:21).

THE RESURRECTION AND THE ESCHATON

The resurrection shows God's vindication of Jesus and reveals our own destiny. God has not abandoned Jesus to Sheol but raised him to life. It shows that God's love is stronger than death for those who cling to him in faith. Jesus is the "first fruits" of the resurrection of the dead (1 Cor 15:20), the hope of all who live in communion with God, and a sign of God's solidarity with all the forgotten victims of history. In Jesus' risen life, the *eschaton* or end time has already appeared, and we look forward to the day when "every sovereignty and every authority and power" and death itself has been destroyed (1 Cor 15:24, 26, NAB). Jesus lives in God's presence, but because he is no longer limited by the boundaries of space and time, he can be equally present to us.

INTERPRETING THE STORY OF JESUS

The early Christians, who of course were all Jews, drew on their sacred texts, the Hebrew Scriptures, to express their faith in Jesus, the Risen One. In the process they used many titles, at least one given to Jesus during his ministry, most used in their preaching after his resurrection. Among them, Jesus was called teacher, prophet, Messiah, Son of Man, Son of David, Son of God, Lord, and occasionally even God. Here I would like to consider three of his most important titles: Messiah, Son of God, and Lord. Afterward, we will see how they were used by Paul and the evangelists in interpreting the story of Jesus.

MESSIAH

The Hebrew *Mashiah* means "anointed"; the Greek *Christos* is a participle meaning "having been anointed." It has the same root as the Greek *chrisma*, ointment, oil, which survives in the English "holy chrism" used in the sacraments. In Israel, kings and priests were anointed.

The Hebrew idea of a future anointed one or messiah goes back to the Oracle of Nathan, in which Nathan at first responds positively to David's desire to build a Temple for God, only to learn in a dream that God does not want David to build the Temple. But honoring David's piety, God makes an extraordinary promise to him through the prophet:

> Moreover the LORD declares to you that the LORD will make you a house. When your days are fulfilled and you lie down with your ancestors, I will raise up your offspring after you, who shall come forth from your body, and I will establish his kingdom. He shall build a house for my name, and I will establish the throne of his kingdom forever. I will be a father to him, and he shall be a son to me. When he commits iniquity, I will punish him with a rod such as mortals use, with blows inflicted by human beings....Your house and your kingdom shall be made sure forever before me; your throne shall be established forever. (2 Sam 7:11–14, 16)

In this prophecy God promises David a son who will build the Temple. God will be a father to this future king, and he will inherit an everlasting kingdom. In its historical meaning, the oracle refers to David son's Solomon, who built the Temple. But it also became the official theology of David's kingdom, the southern kingdom of Judea, leading to a false confidence in God's protection in spite of the people's lack of fidelity to the covenant.

But the image of a future anointed who would be an agent of God's saving power in the life of the people remained popular (see Isa 9:16; Jer 23:5; Mic 5:1–5; Ezek 37:24; Zech 9:9). This future king or "son of David" would be an ideal ruler who would judge the people wisely, bringing justice for the poor and a new era of righteous. In one famous passage in Isaiah 11:1–11, this "shoot from the stump of Jesse" (ESV) will have the spirit of the Lord rest upon him and judge the poor with justice. Thus justice became a characteristic of the messianic age. The second half of this oracle becomes more eschatological, looking forward to a universal reign of peace, with the lion eating hay like the ox, in other words, a restoration of the idyllic condition of the Garden of Eden.

Messiah may have been one of the earliest titles for Jesus; Mark suggests that Peter so identified Jesus, though Jesus ordered him to keep it quiet, probably because some in his day looked forward to a messiah who would lead them in a revolt against the occupying Roman army.

SON OF GOD

The title Son of God could be described as the root metaphor for Jesus in the Gospels, though it can have a number of rather different meanings. Originally the title "Son of God" referred to the son of David, who God promised to adopt as a father and consider as a son (2 Sam 7:14). Some see the words spoken from heaven at the baptism of Jesus, "You are my Son, the Beloved" (Mark 1:11), in this sense. Son of God was also used of angels (Job 1:6; 2:1) and of the "just one" in the Book of Wisdom who claimed God as his Father, only to be condemned to a shameful death by the wicked, waiting to see if God would deliver him (Wis 2:13–18). It is fascinating to wonder if Jesus himself was aware of this very late tradition that so closely parallels his own experience.

What is clear is that Jesus as early as the Q tradition spoke of himself as son and used the intimate Aramaic family term *abba*, "father," in his prayer, something no Jew of his day would have presumed to do. This suggests that he saw his own relationship to God in filial terms. The story of the virginal conception of Jesus (Matt 1:20; Luke 1:34–35) also implies that he is God's son in a unique way, conceived not by normal intercourse but by the Holy Spirit. The Letter to the Hebrews speaks of Jesus as God's final way of addressing his people, no longer through prophets, but through a son who is "heir of all things and through whom he created the universe" (Heb 1:2, NAB). The Gospel of John stresses Jesus' union with the Father and several times addresses him as "the Messiah, the Son of God" (John 11:27; 20:31).

LORD

Perhaps the most significant of the early Jewish Christian titles for Jesus was Lord, the word used in the Septuagint Greek version of the Hebrew Scriptures to translate the holy name Yahweh. It comes from the Greek *kyrios* (Latin *Dominus*, used to address the emperor with intimations of divinity). Wherever "Lord" appears in the Old Testament, we know that the Hebrew text refers to God as Yahweh. In other words, for Greek-speaking Jews, *kyrios* substituted for God's name.

From the earliest days, the Palestinian Jewish Christians referred to Jesus as Lord, using the Aramaic *Mar*, traces of which are evident in Paul, for example, the Aramaic excla-mation *Maran atha*, "Our Lord, come," as well as "the Lord has come" (1 Cor 16:22; cf. *Didachē* 10:6; Rev 22:20). The fact that Paul does not have to translate *Mar* is evidence that Jesus was referred to as Lord even before Paul, while his Greek-speaking Christians confessed Jesus as *kyrios*, Lord (Rom 10:9; 1 Cor 12:3; Phil 2:11).[4] This means that from the beginning the early Jewish Christians were addressing Jesus with a title that, in the Greek translation of the Old Testa-ment, was used for God.

How did the early Christians understand what God had done in the life, death, and resurrection of Jesus? They had many ways of expressing their Easter faith, drawn from their Jewish tradition. Very early they spoke of Jesus' death as a sacrifice for the forgiveness of sins. This is evident in a pre-Pauline proclamation of the witnesses to the resurrection, cited by Paul in his First Letter to the Corinthians (1 Cor 15:3–7), though the sacrificial dimension of Jesus' death is already present in Jesus' words over the bread and the cup at the Last Supper.

Most interesting is the research of Larry Hurtado, who argues that early Christian worship showed a "binitarian pattern" of worship showing Christ as the "recipient of devotion with God and in ways that can be likened only to the worship of a deity."[5] The early Christians prayed to Jesus in the corporate worship or liturgy, addressed him together with God, confessed him as Lord (Rom 10:9–13; 1 Cor 12:3), sang hymns to him, and honored him as living and reigning Lord in their Eucharists.

PAUL

Paul himself has many ways of describing what God had done in the death and resurrection of Jesus. He uses the term "redemption," the paying of a price for someone or something held under a penalty, to express the idea that Christ paid the price for our sins with his blood (Rom 3:23–25; 1 Cor 1:30), or that Christ has "justified" us, made us "righteous" (Rom 4:25; 5:16–18) and so brought about our "reconciliation" with God (Rom 5:10). More important, Paul sees that Jesus' victory over sin means that the power of death has been destroyed (Rom 8) and that those who believe in Jesus will also share in his resurrection. Jesus himself is the "last Adam" (1 Cor 15:45), the "first fruits" of the resurrection from the dead (1 Cor 15:20–23). The author of the letter to the Hebrews speaks of Christ as the mediator of a new covenant and the high priest after the order of Melchizedek whose once and for all sacrifice takes away sin (Heb 7—10).

The New Testament frequently uses the word *salvation* (*sōtēria*) to describe the new life the disciples experienced from God in Christ. Indeed, Jesus' name, *Yeshua*, very common in New Testament times, means "Yahweh is salvation" (Matt 1:21). Derived from the Hebrew root *YŠ*, which has the connotation of space, freedom, and security gained by removing restrictions, *salvation* means "being rescued," "set free," "made whole."

New Testament scholar Luke Timothy Johnson presents a detailed analysis of how salvation was understood by the early Christians. He stresses that this "salvation" was not primarily something hoped for, but something they have already experienced. Thus, they speak of the charge to witness to the ends of the earth and make disciples of all nations. They speak of freedom—from cosmic powers, from oppressive law, and from sin and death. Associated with freedom are the terms *deliverance*, *redemption*, *liberation*, and *salvation*. For these early Christians, salvation was an experience of empowerment, sometimes described as authority (*exousia*), energy (*energeia*), and power (*dynamis*), expressed both in "signs and wonders" and in spiritual transformation. Three terms occur repeatedly in relation to this experience of power: *eternal life*, *forgiveness of sins*, and *Holy Spirit*.[6]

Each evangelist develops a different Christology.

MARK

Mark's Gospel, written around 68, presents Jesus as the Messiah and suffering Son of Man who came, not to be served, but to serve and to give his life as a ransom for many (Mark 10:45). Jesus is proclaimed as Son of God at the beginning of the Gospel, at his baptism, transfiguration, trial before the Sanhedrin, and by the centurion after his death on the cross. Without a Christmas story, it's difficult to read these titles as more than the idea that God adopts or declares Jesus as his son at his baptism. Mark sees Jesus as Son of God in a functional rather than metaphysical sense.

But there are moments when Mark suggests that Jesus is considerably more. Jesus addresses God as *Abba*, "father," something virtually unprecedented for a Jew of the time. The unclean spirits recognize Jesus' true identity (Mark 1:24; 3:11; 5:7). The story of Jesus walking on the water is clearly a theophany; it is Yahweh who walks on the water in the Old Testament (Ps 77:20; Job 9:8). Further, there is the strange verse as Jesus is approaching the disciples, "He intended to pass them by" (Mark 6:48), echoed in Job 9:11, which describes God walking on the waters, saying "should he pass by, I am not aware of him" (Job 9:11, NAB). Other examples include the Transfiguration and what seems to be literally an "I AM" passage in Mark 6:50, reflecting the divine revelatory formula in Exodus 3:14. Mark's Christology is one in process.

MATTHEW

Probably written in the mid-eighties, Matthew's Gospel was addressed to the church in Antioch, which was changing from a largely Jewish Christian congregation to one increasingly comprising Gentile Christians. Thus, the author of the Gospel demonstrates that the coming of the Gentiles represents the fulfillment of the Jewish Scriptures. He quotes the Old Testament more than any other evangelist, presenting Jesus as a teacher like Moses, arranging his sayings into five great discourses to parallel the five books of the Torah or Law.

He sees Jesus as the Messiah in the line of David, the fulfillment of the Law and the prophets. His Christology is considerably higher than either that of Mark or the Q source, focusing on the titles "Son of Man" and "Son of God." The infancy narrative in Matthew includes the story of Jesus' conception by the Holy Spirit and the angel calling him Emmanuel or "God is with us" (Matt 1:23). Jesus is Son of God from his conception. His identity is no longer hidden. Unlike in Mark, where Jesus tells Peter not to tell anyone that he is the Messiah (Mark 8:29–30), in Matthew, Peter responds, "'You are the Messiah, the Son of the living God.' And Jesus answered him, 'Blessed are you, Simon son of Jonah! For flesh and blood has not revealed this to you, but my Father in heaven. And I tell you, you are Peter, and on this rock I will build my church, and the gates of Hades will not prevail against it'" (Matt 16:16–18). Three times Jesus in Matthew refers to himself as "the Son" (Matt 11:27; 21:37; 24:36); he frequently refers to God as "my Father," and once to the Son of Man coming "in the glory of his Father" (Matt 16:27).

LUKE

Luke, also written in the mid-eighties, does not show the disciples confessing Jesus as Son of God during his ministry, but they frequently refer to him as *kyrios* or Lord. Some scholars see Luke's two-volume work, the Gospel of Luke and Acts, as following a two-stage narrative Christology, a Spirit Christology from the time of his conception and throughout his ministry, concluding with his exalted reign (Luke 24:26; Acts 2:33).[7] While there is no suggestion of Jesus' preexistence, he acts in the power of the Spirit; God is working in and through him. His ministry is best summed up by the word *salvation*. In preaching the kingdom of God, Jesus offers forgiveness of sin, drives out evil spirits, heals people, welcomes the marginalized, and after his resurrection, pours out the Holy Spirit.

JOHN

The last Gospel written, John, probably about 95–100, has the highest Christology, a full-blown Christology of pre-existence and incarnation. It begins with the famous Prologue, an early Christian hymn, identifying Jesus as the Word of God, active in creation:

> In the beginning was the Word, and the Word was with God, and the Word was God. He was in the beginning with God. All things came into being through him, and without him not one thing came into being. (1:1–3)

The Prologue concludes with the becoming flesh of the Word:

> And the Word became flesh and lived among us, and we have seen his glory, the glory as of the father's only Son, full of grace and truth. (1:14)

Based on late Old Testament Wisdom theology, the Prologue substitutes the Greek *logos*, "Word," for *Sophia*, "wisdom" (cf. Prov 3; 8:35).

But beyond the Prologue, the Fourth Gospel has other ways of affirming Jesus' divinity and union with the Father. Jesus speaks repeatedly of himself as the Son (John 3:16, 17; 5:20, 21; 6:40; 14:13) and openly proclaims his divine origin (John 8:42) and unity with the Father (John 10:30, 38; 14:9). He repeatedly uses the divine formula "I AM," the Greek *ego eimi* used in the Septuagint to translate the Hebrew formula "I am Yahweh" (Exod 3:14; Isa 43:10), occasionally in the absolute sense, as in "When you lift up the Son of Man, then you will realize that I AM" (John 8:28; cf. 8:58; 13:19). Finally, after Jesus appears to the skeptical Thomas, he confesses "My Lord and my God," one of the few occasions in the New Testament when the word *theos*, "God," is predicated of Jesus (John 20:28; cf. John 1:1; Heb 1:8–9).

CONCLUSION

The disciples were transformed by their Easter experience of the risen Jesus. These men had abandoned him to his fate; Peter had denied him. Only the women had remained at the cross. While the Easter experience of the disciples remains somewhat mysterious, there is a lesson for us there. Jesus appeared, not to the hostile authorities who had closed their hearts to his message, but to those who had been of his company, followed him, and loved him. He offered them forgiveness, the gift of peace, and a share in his mission. He sent them forth to witness to his resurrection, to preach reconciliation, to teach, to baptize, and to forgive sins. He made Peter the pastor of his flock. Saul of Tarsus, who had persecuted his fellow Jews who were followers of Jesus, himself encountered the Risen One and was transformed, becoming the great Apostle of the Gentiles.

It was this experience of new life and the power of the Spirit, reflected in the evangelical and apostolic writings that would be called the New Testament, which led the early Christians to shift their focus from Jesus' preaching the kingdom of God to Jesus himself. They grasped implicitly the intrinsic connection between Jesus and his message. They experienced empowerment, new life, and liberation from oppressive powers, sin, and death. Three terms recur to express their experience: *eternal life*, *forgiveness of sins*, and the *Holy Spirit*.[8]

To interpret the story of Jesus, the first Christians reached into their Jewish tradition. They saw Jesus as the fulfillment of Israel's hope; he was the salvation promised to Israel in the preaching of the prophets, the anointed son of David who would inherit an everlasting kingdom, the new covenant between God and God's people, the wisdom of God come into the world, the first fruits of the resurrection of the dead hoped for late in the Jewish tradition. They called him Messiah, Lord, and Son of God. By the end of the first century, they had established churches around the Mediterranean basin, from Spain to North Africa.

As the church struggled to defend its faith against false teachers and the popular quasi-religious teaching known today as Gnosticism, its Christology became embedded in its creeds. The Apostles' Creed developed in the West from the confession of faith asked of those to be baptized in the church of Rome. An early version is present in the *Apostolic Tradition of Hippolytus*, a text from approximately 215 CE. Versions of the present creed can be found from 340 in Greek and 404 in Latin.

What we call the Nicene-Constantinopolitan Creed developed in the East through the ancient councils. The Council of Nicaea (325), called to counter the erroneous teaching of Arius, affirmed the divinity of Jesus by teaching that he was "consubstantial" (one in being with, of the same substance) with the Father. The Council of Chalcedon (451) safeguarded his humanity, teaching that Jesus was "truly God and truly man, of a rational soul and a body; consubstantial with the Father as regards his divinity, and the same consubstantial with us as regards his humanity, like us in all things but sin" (DS 301). This same period saw the development of the doctrine of the Trinity, with the divinity of the Spirit defined by the Council of Constantinople in 381. We will look at this more closely in the next chapter. The Nicene Creed has remained a standard of Christian faith and is confessed by most churches in their liturgy.

NOTES

1. N. T. Wright, *Jesus and the Victory of God* (Minneapolis, MN: Fortress Press, 1996), 405, cf. 370; see also Walter Kasper, *Jesus the Christ* (New York: Paulist Press, 1977), 117; Raymond E. Brown, *The Death of the Messiah*, vol. 1 (New York: Doubleday, 1994), 460.

2. Joseph Ratzinger, *Eschatology: Death and Eternal Life*, 2nd ed., trans. Michael Waldstein (Washington, DC: Catholic University of America Press, 1988), 90.

3. Gerhard Lohfink, *Jesus of Nazareth: What He Wanted, Who He Was* (Collegeville, MN: Liturgical Press, 2012), 294.

4. See Larry W. Hurtado, *Lord Jesus Christ: Devotion of Jesus in Earliest Christianity* (Grand Rapids, MI: William B. Eerdmans, 2003), 108–14.

5. Ibid., 135.

6. See Luke Timothy Johnson, *The Creed: What Christians Believe and Why It Matters* (New York: Doubleday, 2003), 142–50.

7. See Roger Haight, *Jesus Symbol of God* (Maryknoll, NY: Orbis Books, 1999), 163–68.

8. See Johnson, *The Creed*, 142–50.

PART III

The Holy Spirit

CHAPTER 5

THE HOLY SPIRIT

Jesus broke precedent with his Jewish tradition in speaking of God as *Abba*, father. He also referred to himself as son, suggesting a filial relationship between himself and God. He saw his own ministry as empowered by the Spirit (Mark 3:27–29; Luke 12:10; Matt 12:28) and promised to send the Spirit or Advocate upon his disciples (John 14:16–17; 26; 16:7–8). From the early Christians' conviction of the vivifying presence of the Spirit in the community and their sense that God was revealed in history as Father, Son, and Spirit was developed the doctrine of the Trinity, which is at the heart of the Christian faith.

The Hebrew word for spirit, *rûach*, means "breath," "spirit," "or principle of life," depending on the context. The Greek *pneuma* is similar. In the Old Testament, "spirit" personifies God's creative presence, hovering over the waters at creation (Gen 1:2), empowering the messiah (Isa 11:2; 61:1), looked for as a divine gift to be poured out on all humankind in the messianic age (Joel 2:28). The Spirit is active in the life and ministry of Jesus. He is conceived through the power of the Holy Spirit (Luke 1:35; Matt 1:20); the Spirit descends on him at his baptism (Mark 1:10), leads him into the desert (Luke 4:1), and empowers his ministry (Luke 4:18–19). Luke especially stresses the role of the Spirit in Jesus' ministry.

According to Paul, the risen Christ has become "a life-giving spirit" (1 Cor 15:45). He speaks of "the Spirit of God" or "the Spirit of Christ" or simply "the Spirit" (Rom 8:9–11).

The Spirit is the source of the Christian confession of Jesus as Lord (1 Cor 12:3) and through baptism the Spirit unites the community into one body, breaking down all divisions (1 Cor 12:13). Thus to be "in Christ" is to have new life "in the Spirit," enabling us to know God's love poured into our hearts (Rom 5:5) and to call on God as *Abba* (Rom 8:15). Paul points to the "fruit of the Spirit" in interior dispositions of our lives: "love, joy, peace, patience, kindness, generosity, faithfulness, gentleness, and self-control" (Gal 5:22–23). But in other passages, he speaks of the Spirit in more personal, active terms, scrutinizing the depths of God (1 Cor 2:10), teaching (1 Cor 2:13), leading or guiding (Rom 8:14; Gal 5:18), interceding for members of the church, and helping them pray (Rom 8:26–27). In fact, *spirit* and *grace* are virtually synonymous terms.

The Spirit also symbolizes God's presence and action in the life of the church in the New Testament; Paul describes the church as "a dwelling place of God in the Spirit" (Eph 2:22, NAB), while the Spirit is the church's animating principle. One can speak of the charismatic structure of the church, in which the Spirit pours out a diversity of gifts and ministries (1 Cor 12:4–6).

The personal character of the Spirit is even more evident in John's gospel. Jesus speaks of the "Advocate, the holy Spirit that the Father will send in my name" who will teach you and remind you of everything that I told you (John 14:26, NAB), the Spirit who Jesus will send from the Father to testify to himself (John 15:26).

THE TRINITARIAN MYSTERY

At the heart of the Christian mystery is our share in the life of the triune God who is Father, Son, and Holy Spirit.

The doctrine of the Trinity is not in the New Testament; it was formulated later as the church struggled to develop its theological language, especially in regard to the mystery of Jesus, resulting in the great Nicene-Constantinopolitan Creed, formulated at Nicaea (325) and finalized at Constantinople (381).

TRINITARIAN FORMULAS

If the Creed itself was later, there are various intimations of God's threefold life in the New Testament, expressed in various triadic formulas. For example, as early as 1 Corinthians (written about 56 CE), Paul's description of the variety of gifts and ministries in the church is expressed in trinitarian terms: "There are varieties of gifts, but the same Spirit; and there are varieties of services [*diakonia*], but the same Lord; and there are varieties of activities, but it is the same God who activates all of them in everyone" (1 Cor 12:4–6). He ends his Second Letter to the Corinthians with a blessing still used in the Catholic liturgy: "The grace of the Lord Jesus Christ, the love of God, and the communion of the Holy Spirit be with all of you (2 Cor 13:13). In Matthew's Gospel, Jesus instructs the disciples to "make disciples of all nations, baptizing them in the name of the Father and of the Son and of the Holy Spirit" (Matt 28:19), evidence that the trinitarian baptismal formula was already in place. And there are other formulas that speak of God's salvation in Christ and through the Spirit (2 Cor 1:21–22; Eph 1:13–14; 4:4–6).

In the pre-Nicene church, the focus was always on God's saving work, not on God's inner life. The Spirit was not yet confessed as a distinct personal expression of the Divine. It was only gradually that the doctrine of the Trinity was formulated, as we have noted. But the confession of Jesus as

Lord from the earliest days of the Christian community implied his divine status as well as God's presence and action in the Spirit through his ministry. Jesus was *confessed* as Lord at baptism (Rom 10:8–13), *invoked* as Lord in the Christian assembly (1 Cor 16:22), *worshiped* as Lord (Phil 2:5–11), and *prayed to* for assistance in time of need (Acts 7:59; 2 Cor 12:8).[1] Later in the pre-Nicene period, the prayer and thanksgiving of the church was addressed to the Father in the name of the Lord Jesus Christ, or through him. Origen advised that all prayers be ended "by praising the Father through Jesus Christ in the Holy Spirit" (*On Prayer*, 232), which is still the church's practice today.

DOCTRINE OF THE TRINITY

Theologians today are accustomed to distinguish between the "economic" Trinity, God's self-manifestation *ad extra* in history as Father, Son, and Spirit, and the "immanent" Trinity, God *in se*, in the inner mystery of the divine life, though the distinction has ancient roots. While the pre-Nicene church had stressed the divine *oiconomia* or economy, the struggle with Arius in the early fourth century brought about a shift in both theological language and focus. Arius, reflecting a Greek mindset, saw Jesus as an intermediary between the impassible God and the world of change, a lesser heavenly being, and he popularized his theology with the slogan "there was a time when he was not." As the church fathers struggled with Arius's denial of the divinity of Jesus, they turned increasingly to the inner nature or being of "our lord Jesus Christ." One result was the Council of Nicaea in 325, with its Creed. The other was the formulation of the doctrine of the Trinity.

The Council of Nicaea confessed that Jesus was "of the same substance of" or "one in being with" (*homoousios/*

consubstantial) the Father. Notice the difference in language; the fathers of the council were no longer using the mythopoetic language of scripture, but the more philosophical, ontological categories of the Greco-Roman world. Theology was now, in response to erroneous teaching, speaking of God's inner life, though as Catherine LaCugna notes, the reaction to Arius resulted in a diminished emphasis on Jesus' role as mediator and high priest in his humanity and more on his distance from us as preexistent Christ.[2]

At the same time, some Semi-Arians denied the divinity of the Holy Spirit. Known as the *Pneumatomachoi* or "enemies of the Spirit," they were countered by the work of three great Cappadocians, Basil the Great (330–79), Gregory of Nyssa (335–94), and Gregory of Nazianzus (c. 329–89). It was the latter Gregory who brought their theology to the Council of Constantinople (381), which added to the Creed of Nicaea the confession of the divinity of the Holy Spirit as "the Lord and giver of life, who proceeds from the Father. With the Father and the Son he is worshiped and glorified." In the theology of Augustine, the Spirit is the love that proceeds from the Father and the Son.

THE TRINITY IN EXPERIENCE

Before we conclude this chapter on the Holy Spirit and the mystery of the Trinity, we need to reflect briefly on how the mystery of God present in the history of salvation enters our own experience. Can we experience God as Father, Son, and Spirit?

Some Christians have erroneously suggested that God works sequentially in human history: first, the Father in the work of creation; then the Son, who becomes man in the mystery of the incarnation to accomplish our salvation; and finally the Spirit, empowering and sanctifying the redeemed. But this reduces the divine Persons to moments in the historical manifestation of God. It also tends to make the incarnation the result of sin rather than the divine self-disclosure in the humanity of Jesus. In the early church, this was the heresy known as modalism (or sometimes as Sabellianism or monarchianism).

It makes much more sense theologically to see creation as ongoing, nature as both damaged by sin and graced, and the Spirit gathering us now and in the future into the paschal mystery of Christ's dying and rising to everlasting life. Creation is not an event in the past; if God were not sustaining us in this very instant, we would simply cease to exist. Nor is salvation only a future event, individualistically understood as our being "saved" and entering into bliss. Salvation is God's grace transforming us now and giving us in the Spirit a participation in the divine life. To see human nature as "totally corrupt" because of original sin is to fall into an extreme Calvinist position that fails to recognize that nature is also graced.

The three divine Persons cannot be understood as three independent selves, persons in the modern psychological sense; this comes close to a tritheism. But neither can theology dispense with the language of three Persons. Irenaeus of Lyons (ca. 180) spoke of God's creating and redeeming through his "hands," that is, the Son and the Spirit,[3] emphasizing that God as Father, Son, and Spirit is involved in both works. In more technical trinitarian language, the Greek word *perichoresis*, "circumincession" or "interpenetration," refers to the mutual indwelling of the divine Persons.

Michael Downey speaks of the doctrine of the Trinity as a kind of grammar that, like all grammars, provides rules or parameters within which the truth may be sought. "The term 'person' when used of God is a way of saying that God is always toward and for the other in the self-giving which is constitutive of love. Self-giving is always in relation to another, to others."[4] Thus, relationality is at the very heart of the Christian understanding of God.

Just as the Divine Mystery is best understood as a communion of Persons, one in three, so too, each human person is ordered by nature toward communion with others and that Other who is God. Communion is the source of our happiness and fulfillment; without it, we remain isolated and alone. But we are not alone. The transcendent God is also immanent, and we find in our experience evidence of God's presence as Father, Son, and Spirit. So we might ask, how do we experience this triune God?

THE FATHER

The Father speaks in silence. We become aware of God's presence, beyond image and word, quiet, reassuring. We know that we have been touched, that we are not alone. The Father's presence is comforting, sustaining, and life-giving. It brings a deep sense of peace. But the very taste of God awakens a deeper hunger, a desire for more, for some way to move beyond the veil, to see God's face. In his *Spiritual Exercises*, Ignatius of Loyola describes the grace of the First Week; after reflecting on God's mercy and our own sinfulness, we experience that we are forgiven sinners.

The created world is a kind of sacrament, reflecting the majesty of its creator (Rom 1:20). The blue of the afternoon sky draws us up and out of ourselves and into its vastness. We feel God's comforting touch in the warmth of the sun or the freshness of the rain. We taste God's sweetness in the rich smell of the earth. We rejoice in the exuberance and variety of God's creatures, bursting with life (Ps 104), from the sparrow chirping outside our window to the tiny baby who clings so tightly to our finger. We experience God's love in the touch of a friend. The nighttime canopy of stars suggests a presence that is mysterious and yet near. Thus God bridges the distance between creature and creator.

THE SON

The Son's presence is more challenging. Jesus has a voice. We know him from the gospels; we strive to make his words our own and to imitate his example. His words are not always comforting. He calls us to conversion and to service. He tells us we must lose our life to save it, that the last shall be first, that we must carry our cross with him, that we can embrace him in the poor. For some, his message is too challenging; it threatens our complacency.

Jesus has a claim on us, and we on him. The relation is mutual and personal. He asks us to follow him. He is the way, and the truth, and the life. We experience him as Lord. We ask for strength, for mercy, for forgiveness, and we sense that he has taken away our sins. In him we have been pardoned and set free. Thus to be "in Christ" is to be a "new creation" (2 Cor 5:17).

Christ also has a body, both sacramental and ecclesial. To be "in Christ," a phrase that occurs 216 times in the Pauline letters, is to be in the church, the community of disciples joined to God's people of the first covenant (Gal 3:26–27). The church mediates the presence of the Risen One in word, ministry, communion, and sacrament. The Eucharist is at the center of Catholic faith, uniting us intimately with Jesus and with one another in a holy communion. Who would know Jesus without the church?

THE SPIRIT

The Spirit breathes in our hearts; it is not itself an object of our consciousness. We recognize the Spirit's presence reflexively in our interior lives; we "discern" its presence. The Spirit inspires and animates; sometimes it fills us. The Spirit is the living source of our faith. We find that even in our doubts, we are convinced that God is real, that we are able to call on God as *Abba* (Rom 8:15), confess Jesus as Lord (1 Cor 12:3), and know that our sins have been forgiven (Rom 6:20–23). We experience the "fruit of the Spirit [in] love, joy, peace, patience, kindness, generosity, faithfulness, gentleness, and self-control" (Gal 5:22–23). We find a new power to move beyond our personal failings and sins, a freedom to place ourselves into God's hands and to respond in compassion and love to others. Indeed, love is the greatest of the Spirit's gifts (1 Cor 13). Thus we recognize the Spirit's presence in our affectivity.

The Spirit constitutes the community of disciples as church. We are baptized into one body, given gifts of the Spirit and ministries for the common good, and united by our communion in Christ's body and blood (1 Cor 10—12). At the same time, in our communion with Christ, we sense our communion with one another in his Body for the world. Jesus himself prayed for the unity of his disciples, his church, so that the world may believe (John 17:21)

CONCLUSION

Just as breath gives life to the body, so the Spirit brings God's life to God's people. While the Hebrew Scriptures uses the word *Spirit* to personify the divine presence and action, Jesus thought of himself as empowered by the Spirit, evident in his power to heal.[5] The vivifying role of the Spirit was evident from the beginning. As they pondered the relation between Jesus and the Father, the early Christians gradually came to grasp the divinity of the Spirit, as we have seen. The confession of the divinity of the Spirit was added to the Creed of Nicaea by the Council of Constantinople in 381.

The Holy Spirit animates the church, bestowing on the faithful a diversity of service gifts (*charismata*) and ministries and giving them a share in the life of the Trinity. Eastern Christianity has always had a greater sense of the Spirit's role in theology and liturgy, while Western Christianity tends to be more christological than pneumatological in emphasis.

In recent times, the ecumenical movement has helped Western Christians to recover a greater sense for the power of the Holy Spirit, as has the Pentecostal movement, which continues to grow, particularly in the Southern hemisphere. Some speak of a third wave in the history of Christianity. If the first wave was constituted by the historic churches of the first millennium and the second wave by the confessional churches of the Reformation, then the third wave is represented by the evangelical, charismatic, and above all Pentecostal communities. Stressing the charismatic gifts of the Spirit such as tongues, healing, prophecy, and miracle working, Pentecostal Christians grew from 74 million in 1970 to an estimated 497 million by 1997, an increase of 572 percent.

Pentecostalism has also had a great impact on Catholics through the Charismatic Renewal. By the early twenty-first century, the Charismatic Renewal has grown to nearly 120 million participants, with more than 60 percent of them in Latin America. Some speak today of the "Pentecostalization" of the Catholic Church in Latin America. While they "report holding beliefs and having religious experiences that are typical of Pentecostal or spirit-filled movements," they appear able to incorporate renewalist or charismatic practices without displacing their Catholic identity and core beliefs, and most do so without formal participation in Catholic charismatic organizations.[6]

According to Gastón Espinosa, there are actually more Latino Catholic Charismatics than Protestant Pentecostals in Latin America and in the United States,[7] a fact confirmed by my Pentecostal friends. Estimates at the high end are 5.4 million Latinos in the United States who self-identify as Catholic Charismatics, versus 3.8 million Pentecostals. At least one-third of parishes engaged in Hispanic ministry in the United States have charismatic groups or activities.

But Pentecostal Christianity is not the only tradition that stresses our share in the divine life. Mysticism has always been part of the Catholic tradition, though its expression is less enthusiastic; it represents a quiet, imageless, contemplative experience of God's presence. St. Paul spoke guardedly of his own mystical experience (2 Cor 12:1–4), while the tradition is rich in teachers of contemplation and mystical prayer, from the apophatic theology of the late fifth-century Pseudo-Dionysius, the Areopagite, medieval mystics like Francis of Assisi (c. 1181–1226) and Mechtild of Magdeburg (1207–c. 1285), the unknown author of *The Cloud of Unknowing* in the late fourteenth century, Ignatius of Loyola (1491–1556) and Teresa of Avila (1515–82) in the early modern period, down to Thomas Merton in the twentieth century.

NOTES

1. Geoffrey Wainwright, *Doxology: The Praise of God in Worship, Doctrine, and Life* (New York: Oxford University Press, 1980), 47–48, esp. 47.

2. Catherine Mowry LaCugna, *God for Us: The Trinity and Christian Life* (San Francisco: HarperSanFrancisco, 1991), 126.

3. *Adv Haer.* V,1,3; V,28,4.

4. Michael Downey, *Altogether Gift: A Trinitarian Spirituality* (Maryknoll, NY: Orbis Books, 2000), 48–55, esp. 54.

5. James D. G. Dunn, *Jesus and the Spirit* (Philadelphia: Westminster Press, 1975), 63–67.

6. Pew Forum Survey, "Changing Faiths: Latinos and the Transformation of American Religion,"32, http://www.pewforum.org/files/2007/04/hispanics-religion-07-final-mar08.pdf.

7. Gastón Espinosa, "The Impact of Pluralism on Trends in Latin America and U.S. Latino Religions and Society," *Perspectivas: Occasional Papers* 7 (Fall 2003): 16.

PART IV

The Holy Catholic Church

CHAPTER 6

THE CHURCH

In the Judeo-Christian tradition, God's salvation is always mediated through membership in God's holy people, the people of God. From the time of Abraham, God chose a people of his own, Israel, to be a blessing for all the peoples of the earth (Gen 12:3), a light to the nations (Isa 42:6; 49:6). So, too, being a disciple of Jesus means being a member of his movement, his community, the church. This is where we come to know him, in Christ's Body, the church. Thus, knowledge of God cannot be reduced to an interior enlightenment, such as the Gnostic movements in every age have promised; it cannot flow from a privatized piety to my ideas about God or to a concern for ethics, the perennial temptation of liberal theology.

What do we mean when we say *church*? The term originates not from architecture but from theology. The church is the community of the disciples of Jesus and has existed from the time the resurrection of Jesus gathered his scattered disciples together again. The New Testament word for church is *ekklēsia*, from the Greek *ex* and *kaleo*, "those called out," thus "assembly," "congregation," "church." The Greek *ekklēsia* was used in the Septuagint, the Greek translation of the Hebrew Scriptures, to translate the Hebrew *kahal*, as in the "*kahal* Yahweh" or "assembly of Yahweh," thus the formal or liturgical assembly of the people, most often in the Temple for prayer, or used occasionally for the eschatological Israel to appear in the end times. In secular Greek, *ekklēsia* meant a formal assembly of the people for some civic purpose. The English word, *church*, comes ultimately from the German *kirche*, which comes in turn from the Greek *kuriake oikia*, "belonging to the house of the Lord."

The word translated "church," *ekklēsia*, appears only in two passages in the Gospels (Matt 16:18; 18:17), while the expression *kingdom of God* appears about a hundred times in the Synoptic Gospels. *Church* is obviously a post-Pentecost word.

Paul, whose letters are the earliest in the New Testament, uses the word in three senses. He sometimes refers to a house church or "church in their house" (1 Cor 16:19; Phlm 2; Rom 16:5; Col 4:15), from the earliest days when the Christian community would gather in the home of one of its members. His most frequent use is for the local church, "the church of the Thessalonians" (1 Thess 1:1), "the church of God that is in Corinth" (1 Cor 1:2), or "the churches of Galatia" (Gal 1:2). Occasionally he will use the word in an absolute or universal sense, as in "God has appointed in the church first apostles, second prophets, third teachers" (1 Cor 12:28), a usage more common in later letters. Thus the word can be used for the local church, the church in a place, and for the whole or universal church, called the "catholic church" as early as Ignatius of Antioch (c. 110; *Smy* 8).

A summary passage in Luke's Acts of the Apostles, joining Peter's Pentecost sermon with the cure of a cripple, can serve as an outline of what constitutes the church: "Those who welcomed his message were baptized....They devoted themselves to the apostles' teaching and fellowship, to the breaking of bread and the prayers" (Acts 2:41–42). Note the elements of the church's life named here. *Baptism* is the rite of incorporation into the church, following upon acceptance of the word or preaching. The *teaching (didachē) of the apostles* points to the original apostolic witnesses, what will later be called the apostolic tradition. The *breaking of the bread* is Luke's term for the Eucharist (see Luke 24:35); the church has at its heart the Eucharist. The *communal life*, using the term *koinōnia*, to be considered below, speaks of the church as a community. And finally *prayer*, for the church is a community of prayer and worship.

NEW TESTAMENT METAPHORS

Several New Testament metaphors for church can help us better understand the church's nature. Three of the most important include people of God, Body of Christ, and temple of the Spirit. Others are sheepfold (John 10:1ff.), synagogue (Jas 2:2), and the vine and the branches (John 15:1–7).

PEOPLE OF GOD

Originating in the Old Testament, where Israel and God's people are virtually synonymous, people of God is rooted in God's promise to Abraham to make of him "a great nation" through whom all the communities of the earth would be blessed (Gen 12:2–3) and in the covenant that God makes with Israel on Sinai (Exod 20:1–7). The exodus story could be seen as the root metaphor for the establishment of Israel as God's people, while the prophets continued to remind the people of God's promise to "gather" the people, scattered by their violation of the covenant and their sins (Isa 11:12–13; Jer 23:7–8; Ezek 37:21–22).

Jesus, as a man deeply rooted in the religious tradition of his people, was keenly aware of God's promise to "gather" and restore Israel. During his historical ministry, he gathered around him a group of disciples, placing at their center the Twelve, a number symbolic of his desire to establish or reconstitute the eschatological Israel or Israel of salvation. Scholars today refer to this group of men and women as the Jesus Movement; Jesus gave them a share in his own ministry, that is, to heal the sick, cast out demons, and proclaim that the reign of God was at hand (Mark 6:7–13; Luke 10:2–12).[1] His ministry, seeking to gather a renewed Israel and proclaim the nearness of the kingdom of God, was clearly a challenge to the Israel of his day, and ultimately cost him his life.

The church grew out of the Jesus Movement, with its mission of proclaiming the reign of God, its leadership in the persons of the Twelve, and its rituals of baptism and Eucharist. As Gerhard Lohfink has written, "What Jesus founded, when he appointed the Twelve, was not the Church but the eschatological people of God. But in that act of foundation the basis for the Church was prepared. The Church goes back to the actions of Jesus himself."[2] Though the church is only explicitly identified as the people of God in one place (1 Pet 2:10), the idea that these Christian communities have been joined to the people of God in the Jewish Scriptures, indeed that the church represents the eschatological Israel, is implicit throughout the New Testament.

The early Christians of course were all Jews; indeed, the earliest church could be described as a movement within Judaism that took several decades to establish its own separate identity. But as these early Christians appealed to the Hebrew Scriptures to see themselves as the people of God (2 Cor 2:14—3:18; Gal 3:28–29; Heb), they recognized a new covenant established in the blood of Christ poured out for the forgiveness of sins (Mark 14:24; 1 Cor 11:25) and gradually came to realize that salvation in Christ meant that observance of the Mosaic Law was no longer necessary, first for non-Jewish converts, and ultimately for all. The apostle Paul played a major role in this process, but he was not the only one. While people of God is a metaphor for the church, it also implicitly includes Israel as the historic Jewish people, the rich root of the olive tree onto which the Gentiles have been grafted (Rom 11:17–24).

BODY OF CHRIST

The most powerful metaphor for church is Body of Christ, which first appears in Paul's First Letter to the Corinthians, a divided community whose unity he sought to reestablish. Paul stresses how they are one in Christ with a unity established through what the later church would call sacraments. Thus, he tells them that in their communion in the body of Christ through sharing in the one loaf of bread of the Eucharist, they, though many, have become one body, because they all partake of the one loaf (1 Cor 10:16–17). Two chapters later he argues that "in the one Spirit we were all baptized into one body—Jews or Greeks, slaves or free— and we were all made to drink of one Spirit (1 Cor 12:13; cf. Gal 3:27–29). Baptism and Eucharist unite the disciples into one body, breaking down divisions between and among them. Still later he says, "Now you are the body of Christ and individually members of it" (1 Cor 12:27). Note that he does not say one body *in* Christ, but simply you are Christ's body, the one body *of* Christ.

The term *body* was used in Hellenistic culture as a political or inclusive metaphor for diverse elements. While Paul would have been familiar with that usage, he may have derived his metaphor from the Lord's Supper, with its emphasis on the body and blood of the Lord (1 Cor 11:27–29). But the metaphor of the church as the Body of Christ has a deeper meaning today. Body is what makes spirit visible, as anyone sensitive to body language knows instinctively. Teachers know this; they can tell at a glance when a class is engaged and attentive, or when the students have tuned out, their eyes glazed or wandering. As body makes spirit visible, so also the church as the Body of Christ makes visible the risen Jesus, who is no longer here in his earthly mode of existence.

How could anyone come to know Jesus today without his Body the church? The church mediates Christ's presence and action. It is the church in its self-actualization, in its preaching (*kerygma*), teaching (*didachē*), worship (*liturgia*), ministry (*diakonia*), and communion or fellowship (*koinōnia*) that makes Christ visible and accessible today. Scripture alone is not enough; scripture needs a community that lives, celebrates, and proclaims the story of Jesus to bring him to others. Colossians and Ephesians further develop the metaphor, applying it to the church, though now understood in a universal sense. Christ is the head of his Body, the church (Col 1:18; 2:19; Eph 5:23), the source of its growth (Col 2:19; Eph 4:16), building it up through ministry (Eph 4:12). Note that the author here is using *ekklēsia* in the sense of the whole or universal church. In other words, the Body of Christ is not just the local congregation; it is the whole church, a point with important ecumenical implications.

TEMPLE OF THE SPIRIT

A third metaphor sees the church as a temple of the Spirit. Paul has a strong sense of the Spirit's vivifying presence in the church and its members, bringing them to faith in Christ (1 Cor 12:3), enabling them to know God's love poured out (Rom 5:5), calling on God as *Abba* (Rom 8:15), and looking forward to the resurrection (Rom 8:11).

Thus the author of Ephesians (the letter is most probably Deutero-Pauline) speaks of the church as "the household of God, built upon the foundation of the apostles and prophets, with Christ Jesus himself as the cornerstone. In him the whole structure is joined together and grows into a holy temple in the Lord; in whom you also are built together spiritually into a dwelling place for God" (Eph 2:19–22). In the Acts of the Apostles, Luke stresses the role of the Spirit in the life of the church, beginning with the great event of Pentecost (Acts 2:1–4) and showing how the Spirit guides the church. In John, also, the Spirit or Advocate guides the community, reminding its members of what Jesus has taught them (John 14:25; 15:26; 16:13).

THE CONCEPT OF COMMUNION

One of the most important concepts for the Catholic theology of the church (ecclesiology) to emerge since Vatican II is the concept of *koinōnia* or communion.[3] From the Greek *koinos*, or "common," *koinōnia* means "a sharing or participation in something else." Appearing nineteen times in the New Testament, it is generally translated as "communion" or "fellowship." Protestants prefer "fellowship"; Catholics, because of its sacramental and ecclesial connotations, prefer "communion."

The term was first used by Paul, who sees Christian life as a participation in a common life in Christ and with one another, all of this a gift of God. Thus, he says, "God is faithful; by him you were called into the fellowship (*koinōnia*) of his Son, Jesus Christ our Lord (1 Cor 1:9). Communion takes place through sharing (*koinōnia*) in the gospel (Phil 1:5), in faith (Phlm 6), in the suffering of Christ (Phil 3:10; 2 Cor 1:7), and in his Spirit (2 Cor 13:13). Luke uses *koinōnia* to describe the communal life of the community, as we have seen (Acts 2:42). The First Letter of John uses the term to describe our shared life with God and with one another:

> We declare to you what we have seen and heard so that you also may have fellowship (*koinōnia*) with us; and truly our fellowship (*koinōnia*) is with the Father and with his Son Jesus Christ. (1 John 1:3; cf. vv. 6, 7)

Therefore, *koinōnia* means more than simply fellowship; it means a participation in the divine life. The author of 2 Peter goes so far as to say that through God's promises "you may come to share (*koinōnoi*) in the divine nature" (2 Pet 1:4, NAB).

There is a sacramental dimension to *koinōnia*. As we have seen, Paul speaks of our communion in the body and blood of Christ in the Eucharist as constituting the church as the Body of Christ: "The cup of blessing that we bless, is it not a sharing (*koinōnia*) in the blood of Christ? The bread that we break, is it not a sharing (*koinōnia*) in the body of Christ? Because there is one bread, we who are many are one body, for we all partake of the one bread" (1 Cor 10:16–17).

Koinōnia, or communion, is more than an invisible reality; it is always expressed by visible signs. Paul and Barnabas received from the "pillars" of the church, James, Kephas (Peter), and John, "their right hands in partnership (*koinōnias*)," signifying approval of their preaching of the gospel to the Gentiles (Gal 2:9). Throughout the first millennium, the communion of the churches was expressed through visible signs such as eucharistic hospitality, letters of communion, communion among the bishops themselves, the participation of at least three bishops in the ordination of a new bishop, and as early as the third century, communion with the bishop of Rome or pope.[4] One interesting sign was the *fermentum*, the sending of a piece of the consecrated eucharistic bread from the bishop or pope's Eucharist to be consumed by priests or bishops in a neighboring church as a sign of communion. A vestige of this practice remains in the Catholic Mass, where the priest, before receiving communion, breaks off a small piece of the host and drops it into the chalice.

The term *communion* is used in various senses today. We speak of a person's communion with the church, expressed by participating in the Eucharist (holy communion), and also of excommunication, a penalty for some serious offense injurious to the communion of the church (see 1 Cor 5:2). Communion among some churches was lost, first between the Greek-speaking Eastern and Latin Western church in 1054, and again as a result of the Reformation in the sixteenth century. The goal of the ecumenical movement is not the creation of a mega-church but the restoration of communion between and among the different churches. The expression *communio sanctorum* refers to the communion of saints, who share in God's life and are still in communion with us, making possible the ancient practice of asking their intercession. Originally, *communio sanctorum* meant "communion in holy things," Christ's saving grace mediated through baptism and Eucharist.

EARLY CATHOLICISM

The Christian communities of the apostolic age had a diversity of "charismatic" gifts (*charismata*) and ministries (*diakoniai*), most evident in 1 Corinthians 12—14, with the Twelve serving as a kind of council, consulted for major decisions affecting the whole community (see Acts 6:1–7; 15:1–29; Gal 2:1–10). But by the year 70 CE, marked by the destruction of the Temple in Jerusalem, the members of the Twelve had died or been killed. For example, Peter was crucified in the year 63 in connection with Nero's persecution, and Paul was put to death by the year 67. In the period after the year

70, sometimes referred to as the postapostolic age, the church began to go through a process of institutionalization.

With the original witnesses to the ministry of Jesus gone from the scene, there is an emphasis in the letters and books from this postapostolic period on safeguarding the apostolic tradition; warnings about false teachers; a ritual for the transmission of office through the laying on of hands, later known as ordination; the presiding office of the presbyter/ bishops, in the process of developing into the threefold ministry of a bishop, assisted by presbyters (from which the English word *priest* is derived) and deacons; and finally an emphasis on these leaders as succeeding to the place of the apostles, later called the apostolic succession.

For example, the author of 1 Timothy refers to "elders [*presbuteroi*] who rule well be[ing] considered worthy of double honor, especially those who labor in preaching and teaching" (1 Tim 5:17). The word translated here as "honor," *timēs*, means "compensation," as the following verse about a worker deserving his pay illustrates; in other words, these are salaried ministers whose duties include both preaching and teaching. Similarly, the First Letter of Peter, written some twenty years after Peter's death, exhorts the presbyters of the churches in Asia Minor as a "fellow presbyter" (1 Pet 5:1–4, NAB), and Paul addresses the presbyters who will succeed him at Miletus to shepherd the flock in which the Holy Spirit has made them "overseers" (*episkopous*, "bishops"), keeping them faithful to the truth they have received (Acts 20:28–30).

The Lutheran scholar Ernst Käsemann characterizes these writings as representing "early Catholicism," among them Colossians and Ephesians, 1 and 2 Timothy, Titus, Acts, Jude, 2 Peter, and the Johannine Letters as well as non-canonical works from the same period such as the *Didachē* (c. 96) and the letters of Ignatius of Antioch (110).

Käsemann, of course, rejects this development as an effort to bind the Spirit to an emerging institutionalized office, and thus an attempt to limit grace.[5] But it was precisely these structures that kept the churches together, under episcopal leadership and united in faith. The threefold ministry of a bishop, assisted by presbyters and deacons, was in place at Antioch and in some other churches by the end of the first century. By the end of the second century, it was in place throughout the church. It was this church, called "catholic" by Ignatius of Antioch, that was responsible for the handing on and canonizing of the New Testament. Today it could be described as the world's oldest institution.

BAPTISM

The English word *baptism* is derived from the Greek *baptismos*, meaning "a ritual washing." The church from the beginning adopted this rite, practiced by John the Baptist and apparently by Jesus and his disciples in the early days of his ministry (John 3:22). But while John's baptism was a sign of repentance, Christian baptism took on a very different meaning, with different New Testament authors stressing different aspects of the rite.

PAUL

Paul has perhaps the most developed theology of baptism. First, baptism incorporates a person into Christ's paschal mystery of dying and rising to new life. Paul writes: "Do you not know that all of us who have been baptized into Christ Jesus were baptized into his death? Therefore we have been buried with him by baptism into death, so that, just as Christ was raised from the dead by the glory of the Father, so we too might walk in newness of life" (Rom 6:3–4). The paschal mystery, sharing in Christ's passage through death in union with the Father to life, is at the heart of the Christian mystery. At the beginning of the Catholic funeral rite, the priest places a white pall over the casket and recalls these words about baptism into the mystery of Christ's death so that the deceased might also share in the resurrection.

Second, baptism unites the church as the Body of Christ: "For just as the body is one and has many members, and all the members of the body, though many, are one body, so it is with Christ. For in the one Spirit we were all baptized into one body—Jews or Greeks, slaves or free—and we were all made to drink of one Spirit" (1 Cor 12:12–13). In a beautiful expression, he says in Galatians to those baptized that you "have clothed yourselves with Christ" (Gal 3:27). They have put on Christ like a garment, like the white garment so often worn in the ceremony of baptism. And as a result, "There is no longer Jew or Greek, there is no longer slave or free, there is no longer male and female; for all of you are one in Christ Jesus" (Gal 3:28). Thus, baptism breaks down all divisions within the Christian community, whether based on race, ethnicity, gender, sexual orientation, or social status. It has never been easy for the church to be what it must be, a community of disciples; it has often fallen short of the unity that comes from baptism.

LUKE

For Luke, baptism is contingent upon acceptance of the apostolic preaching and serves to incorporate one into the community of the church (Acts 2:41). Thus it is a sacrament of initiation and presumes a coming to faith on the part of the person baptized. It is primarily a sacrament for adults. Christians have differed about infant baptism throughout history; the Anabaptists in the sixteenth-century Reformation and some churches today insist that baptism demands faith, and therefore they do not baptize infants or children. Others, with equal reason, insist that from the earliest days whole families were baptized when they accepted the faith, as in the story of Cornelius (Acts 10:47).

Both positions can be supported with solid reasons, and those from each tradition should respect the other. What does not make sense is baptizing infants when there is no practice of the faith in the home, no "domestic church," to use a term that goes back to the fourth century. Such "indiscriminate" baptism risks turning what should be the sacramental moment of baptism into a mere rite of passage. Evangelical Christians rightly object that many Catholics and others from mainline churches have been sacramentalized but not evangelized, contributing to even more baptized nonbelievers in our secular world. The canon law of the Catholic Church says that when there is no hope that the infant will be brought up in the faith, the baptism is to be put off (canon 868, 2) until there is some hope of practice.

JOHN

John's theology of baptism emerges in Jesus' dialogue with Nicodemus. He tells Nicodemus that no one can enter the kingdom of God without being born from above, which Nicodemus misunderstands as having to reenter his mother's womb and being born again (John 3:3–4). Jesus responds that "no one can enter the kingdom of God without being born of water and Spirit," obviously talking of baptism (John 3:5). Jesus speaks here of a spiritual rebirth, mediated by sacramental incorporation into the community of the church.

Evangelical Christians have seen in this text a warrant for their emphasis on being "born again," though what the text actually says is being born from above. But the metaphor is a good one; baptism should bring about a new birth, a spiritual regeneration, a significant change in a person's life. Baptism presupposes a genuine conversion; it means that after the sacrament one's life is going to be different.

ECCLESIAL LIFE

How does baptism mediate God's grace in the real order of things? It is not something that happens automatically, by magic, so to speak. Incorporation into the Christian community means moving from a world still under the rule of sin to one in which the disciples of Jesus are living in his Spirit; it means a significant change in relationships. Relationships are real; they shape and form us. We live in a damaged world; of this there is obvious evidence. It is a world too often marked by violence and injustice, racism and prejudice, selfishness and a lack of concern for others. Too many are desperately poor, held in bondage by unjust structures and the abuse of power. Our cultures transmit inherited prejudices from one generation to another; our families are often dysfunctional. Think about the lifetime disadvantages experienced by a child who comes from a dysfunctional family, the difficulty he or she has in becoming a free and responsible person with a sense of personal value.

We know we feel differently about ourselves when we are in love and see ourselves reflected in the eyes of the beloved. We are empowered and come to a new appreciation of ourselves. Similarly, the church is a community in which Christ and his liberating gospel are proclaimed; people are taught about Jesus, worship him, minister to others, and experience communion in his name. The church lives in the Spirit of Jesus, and communicates that to others. It is his body for the world.

EUCHARIST

The Eucharist is known by many names. Protestants often refer to it as the Lord's Supper; Anglicans call it holy communion; Orthodox the divine liturgy or *Synaxis* ("assembly"). Catholics call it the Mass, the liturgy, or most often, the Eucharist. Like the Jewish Passover supper, the Eucharist is a ritual meal that recalls and makes present God's saving event through narrative and ritual. The great Eucharistic Prayer proclaims Christ's life, death, and resurrection and the assembled community participates in this mystery by sharing in the bread blessed and the wine poured out, confessed in faith as his body and blood. The antecedents of the Eucharistic Prayer are to be found in the Jewish grace after meals or *birkat hamazon*, prayed by the host in thanksgiving. The biblical roots of the Eucharist are to be found in the image of the rich feast or banquet symbolizing God's salvation and in the table-fellowship tradition of Jesus, transformed in light of the Last Supper. The following texts stand out.

ESCHATOLOGICAL BANQUET

Isaiah foretells a great feast of rich food and choice wines on the mountain in the heavenly Jerusalem when God's reign is revealed to all peoples and death itself is destroyed (Isa 25:6–8). In Matthew 8:10–12, Jesus uses this image to foreshadow the banquet in the kingdom of heaven, when many will come from the East and the West to recline with Abraham, Isaac, and Joseph (cf. Luke 13:26–30). The banquet is sometimes presented as a wedding feast (Matt 22:1–14; cf. Luke 14:15–24).

TABLE-FELLOWSHIP TRADITION

Much of Jesus' ministry took place at meals; he dined in the houses of Pharisees and religious leaders, shared meals with his disciples and with the multitude, and went out of his way to include those marginalized by the religious community, the "tax collectors and sinners" (Mark 2:16), for which he was criticized as "a glutton and a drunkard" (Matt 11:19). The story of the miracle of the loaves, told twice in Mark and Matthew, belongs to this tradition; Jesus miraculously feeds the vast crowd that followed him, multiplying the bread and the fish (Mark 6:34–44; 8:1–9; Matt 14:13–21; 15:32–39). The telling of the story in the Gospels takes on eucharistic connotations, using the liturgical formula still used in the liturgy: "Taking the seven loaves he gave thanks, broke them, and gave them to his disciples to distribute" (Mark 8:6, NAB).

LAST SUPPER NARRATIVES

The table-fellowship tradition takes on a new dimension at the Last Supper, when Jesus identified the bread and wine of the table with his imminent death on the cross: "This is my body that is for you....This cup is the new covenant in my blood" (1 Cor 11:24–25). Paul's and Luke's versions of this "institution narrative" contains the command to repeat ("do this in memory of me"), suggesting that the disciples are to continue this ritual meal with the new meaning Jesus has given it the night before he died.

In Luke's story of the two disciples on the road to Emmaus, the risen Jesus himself, as yet unrecognized by the disciples, joins them for supper where he "took bread, blessed and broke it, and gave it to them" (Luke 24:30), whereupon their eyes were opened and they recognized him. Most likely the story comes out of the experience of the earliest Christians, who continued the table-fellowship tradition of the ministry with the new meaning Jesus gave it at the Last Supper, with this meal becoming a moment for recognizing the risen Jesus' presence to the community "in the breaking of the bread," as the church has done ever since.

JOHN'S GOSPEL

While the Fourth Gospel lacks the story of the institution of the Eucharist at the Last Supper, it has perhaps the most literal interpretation of the early church's eucharistic faith of any of the Gospels. The whole sixth chapter is eucharistic, beginning with the story of the multiplication of the loaves, moving from the story of Jesus walking on the sea into the "Bread of Life" discourse, which begins with Jesus as the true bread come down from heaven (John 6:22–51), and moves finally to a specifically eucharistic meaning:

> The Jews then disputed among themselves, saying, "How can this man give us his flesh to eat?" So Jesus said to them, "Very truly, I tell you, unless you eat the flesh of the Son of Man and drink his blood, you have no life in you. Those who eat my flesh and drink my blood have eternal life, and I will raise them up on the last day; for my flesh is true food and my blood is true drink." (John 6:52–56)

Here we have traditional "real presence" language; the bread and wine are the flesh and blood of Jesus, even if in John's account the Jews were not able to accept this. But how do we express the church's faith in Jesus' eucharistic presence in theological language? That raises the question of the meaning of the Eucharist.

MEANING OF THE EUCHARIST

The celebration of the Eucharist embraces the past, present, and future dimensions of our salvation. It looks back to and proclaims the death of Jesus until he comes again (1 Cor 11:26), the symbol of his life as a total offering to the Father, remembering it (*anamnesis*) through narrative and ritual. It recognizes that the risen Jesus is himself present to the community in the breaking of the bread (Luke 24:25), giving himself as food and drink (John 6:55) and uniting the community as his body for the world (1 Cor 10:17). In his body and blood, we have nourishment for eternal life, anticipating the life to come in which we already share (John 6:54).

In its multidimensional meaning, the Eucharist can be described as a memorial of the sacrifice of Christ (the holy sacrifice of the Mass); a prayer of thanksgiving (*eucharistein*, "to give thanks") to the Father, thanking God for the life, death, and resurrection of Jesus and gift of the Spirit; a sacramental meal; a sign of the kingdom, breaking down divisions based on race, ethnicity, social status, or gender, uniting all into Christ's body; and an intimate encounter with the risen Jesus in holy communion.

From the earliest days of the church, Christians have recognized that in the Lord's Supper or Eucharist they truly encounter the risen Jesus, that they receive his body and blood. Catholics speak of this as the "real presence" of Christ; in receiving the bread and wine, they are receiving the body and blood of the Lord. But expressing this deep conviction in appropriate theological language is not always easy. The early Christians did not speak of a "substantial change" in the elements of bread and wine; still less did they use the term *transubstantiation*, which appeared only in the eleventh century.

It makes much more sense to approach this question, not

with the church's latter doctrinal language, but with the experience of the early Christians who recognized Christ's presence in the meal. Paul told the Corinthians that in sharing in the blessed cup and broken bread they had a sharing or communion (*koinōnia*) in the body and blood of Christ (1 Cor 10:16–17). Luke speaks of recognizing the risen Jesus present in the "breaking of the bread" (Luke 24:31, 35; cf. Acts 2:42). John uses very literal language, as we saw earlier, speaking of eating the flesh and drinking the blood of the Son of Man, scandalizing some of the disciples who were unable to accept this teaching and left his company (John 6:54). All of these texts point to Christ's presence in the meal, in the bread and wine.

From the second century on, the fathers of the church used realistic language to describe Christ's eucharistic presence. Ignatius of Antioch (d. 110) argued that the Docetists who denied that Christ was truly a human being (reflecting a Greek prejudice against the material) abstain from the Eucharist (thanksgiving) and prayer because they do not believe that the Eucharist "is the flesh of our Savior Jesus Christ" (*Smy* 6.7). Justin Martyr (d. ca. 165) compared the union of the bread and wine with Christ's body and blood to the joining of the divine and human in the Incarnation (*First Apology*, 66). Ambrose (d. 397) spoke of a change of the elements, arguing that the power of grace was superior to that of nature (*On the Mysteries*, 52).

A theological dispute in the eleventh century led to the introduction of the language of substantial change or transubstantiation. Berengar (d. 1088), a theologian who headed a school at Tours in France, seems to have taught that Christ was present in the Eucharist *only* as a sign, an approach that was seen as overly symbolic. The Council of Rome (1059) imposed an excessively literal formula on Berengar, requiring him to confess that communicants chew on the body of

Christ (a phrase also used by Luther). Today we avoid such literal language.

The Fourth Lateran Council (1215) used the term *transubstantiation* to affirm that while the appearances of the bread and wine remained the same, the substance of both really changed. The Council of Trent adopted this term after the Reformation in the sixteenth century as an "appropriate" (*aptissime*) way of talking about what happens in the Eucharist, but more to the point, it affirmed that in the Eucharist the whole Christ was present, "body and blood, soul and divinity" (DS 1651). In other words, what is present is not discrete flesh and blood but the risen Jesus himself in his glorified humanity. As liturgist Nathan Mitchell has said, "The body of Christ offered to Christians in consecrated bread and wine is not some*thing* but some*one*. In the Eucharist Christ is present not as an 'object' to be admired but as a person (a 'subject') to be encountered."[6]

STRUCTURE

Finally, we need to consider the Eucharist from a liturgical perspective. The eucharistic liturgy is divided into the Liturgy of the Word and the Liturgy of the Eucharist, formerly known as the Mass of the Catechumens and the Mass of the Faithful, as those being instructed, neophytes or catechumens, were present only for the first part, the reading of the Scriptures and the homily before they were led forth by the deacon. The Eucharist was only for the baptized, those who had been fully initiated into the church.

The Liturgy of the Word is built on the Jewish synagogue service, a reading from the Law and the prophets, a homily or reflection on the readings, and some prayers (cf. Luke 4:16–21). The Liturgy of the Eucharist takes its name from the great eucharistic prayer proclaimed by the presiding priest or bishop. After receiving the bread and wine from the congregation, the presider invites all present to give thanks ("Let us give thanks to the Lord our God") in the introductory prayer called appropriately the Preface. Then he gives thanks for God's mighty works, for creation, for sending his Son for our salvation, remembering his words at the Last Supper (*anamnesis*), for his resurrection, ascension, and for the gift of the Holy Spirit. He asks God to send down the Spirit upon the gifts of bread and wine and upon the church (*epiclesis*). The Eucharistic Prayer ends with the people joining in the Great Amen. The final part of the liturgy includes praying together the Lord's Prayer, breaking the bread, communion of the faithful, and a dismissal with a blessing.

CONCLUSION

Just as being a Jew meant being part of God's covenant people, so for Paul, to be "in Christ" is to be a member of his Body, the church. For all his emphasis in Romans and Galatians on our being saved by faith, not by works of the Law, his letters are always to and about churches. Nor can knowledge of God be reduced to some interior feeling or subjective idea of God, lest we risk worshiping a god of our own creation. If the transcendent, unknowable God has broken the silence of the ages and been revealed in the story of the life, death, and resurrection of Jesus, we need the church to proclaim that mystery.

Baptism initiates one into the community of the church. It does not work a magic transformation but, in bringing one into a community of people whose lives have been transformed, the sacrament introduces the person baptized into the community's own shared life of faith in the Spirit. Baptism breaks down divisions between peoples, so that there is no longer Jew or Greek, slave or free, male or female (Gal 3:28; cf. 1 Cor 12:12).

At the center of Catholic life, the Eucharist gives thanks for God's mighty works on behalf of God's people. Sharing in the bread broken and cup poured out, the community enters into an intimate union with Christ; the community members receive his body and blood. In sharing in the one loaf, they themselves become his body for the world. His blood is the blood of the new covenant that Jesus established through his life, death, and resurrection. The church is the people of God, the Body of Christ, a temple in the Spirit, which mediates a share in the life of the Trinity.

Thus, the church mediates God's grace through word, sacrament, and communal life. How could anyone know Christ without the church that continues to proclaim his gospel, celebrates his presence in word and sacrament, and ministers to others in his name? Without an interpreting community that lives out the gospel, the Scriptures would be a "dead letter" or lost to a multiplicity of conflicting interpretations. One cannot be a Christian all by one's self.

NOTES

1. See Terrence W. Tilley, *The Disciples' Jesus: Christology as Reconciling Practice* (Maryknoll, NY: Orbis Books, 2008).

2. Gerhard Lohfink, *Does God Need the Church? Toward a Theology of the People of God* (Collegeville, MN: Liturgical Press, 1999), 163.

3. The concept of *koinōnia* has been used in the work of the Faith and Order Commission, even before the formation of the World Council of Churches in 1948.

4. See Ludwig Hertling, *Communio: Church and Papacy in Early Christianity* (Chicago: Loyola University Press, 1972), 23–36.

5. See Ernst Käsemann, "Paul and Early Catholicism," in *New Testament Questions of Today* (London: SCM Press, 1969), 235–51.

6. Nathan Mitchell, "Who Is at the Table? Reclaiming the Real Presence," *Commonweal* 122 (January 27, 1995): 12.

CHAPTER 7

THE SECOND VATICAN COUNCIL

In the life of the church, there have been three great reforming movements. The first was the Gregorian Reform in the eleventh century, an unintended result of which was the modern, centralized papacy. The second was the Protestant Reformation in the sixteenth century, leading to a multiplicity of churches and traditions that has endured down to the present day. The third was the Second Vatican Council (1962–65).[1] The Council accepted modernity's historical-critical methodology; endorsed the ecumenical movement and the principle of religious liberty, both of which the Catholic Church had previously rejected; and moved out of its post-Reformation defensiveness to see itself at the *world's* service, particularly in its Pastoral Constitution on the Church in the Modern World, *Gaudium et spes*.

The Catholic Church of the mid-twentieth century was to all outward appearances thriving. Catholics were united under the strong leadership of Pope Pius XII; they went to Mass and communion in record numbers, married other Catholics, and rarely questioned the teachings of church authorities. The church's seminaries and religious houses were bursting at the seams, missionary work was flourishing, and Catholics had a clear sense of their religious identity.

At the same time, the church seemed to be stuck in a time warp. With a few exceptions, Catholic scholarship was undistinguished. Theologians whose works were judged dangerous by Roman authorities were routinely disciplined, removed from their positions, or had their books placed on the Index of Prohibited Books. The church was suspicious of the ecumenical movement that had arisen among Protestants, officially rejected by Pope Pius XI's 1928 encyclical *Mortalium Animos*, and Catholics were told not to take part in Protestant services. Laypeople had little role in the church or its liturgy. And in Catholic colleges in the United States, students were reading a book called *The Thirteenth: Greatest of Centuries*, which looked back with nostalgia to the Middle Ages.

CURRENTS OF RENEWAL

Still, there were some currents of renewal flowing beneath the surface that were to reshape Catholicism at the Second Vatican Council. The modern biblical movement, largely the work of Protestant scholars in the largely secular German universities, had been initially rejected by the Vatican's Pontifical Biblical Commission. But to the surprise of many, Pope Pius XII cautiously embraced it in his 1943 encyclical *Divino afflante Spiritu*. From this point on, a more historical-critical approach to biblical studies would become familiar to Catholics, first in seminaries and graduate schools, and then in universities, as Catholic scholars trained in the modern disciplines of form criticism, redaction criticism, text criticism, and source criticism began taking their places in Catholic institutions of higher learning.

Another current of renewal was represented by the liturgical movement. Originating in the nineteenth century in the Benedictine monasteries of Germany, Switzerland, and France, the liturgical movement began by encouraging the

use of Gregorian chant in the liturgy and a greater participation by the faithful, who up to this point had been largely
spectators at a liturgy conducted by priests in a foreign language. Again, Pius XII gave his always cautious support to
the liturgical renewal, first in his encyclical *Mystici corporis*
(1943), with its sacramental view of the church, and more
explicitly in *Mediator Dei* (1947), encouraging the liturgical
movement and the dialogue Mass, in which the people
responded to the priest using the Latin prayers of the liturgy.

Perhaps most important was a movement originating in
France known as the "new theology" (*nouvelle théologie*).
At its heart was a method that became known as *ressourcement*, a "return to the sources" of the church's theology and
worship in the scriptures, the liturgy, and the fathers of the
church. Different from the neo-Scholasticism then dominant
in Catholic theology, an abstract philosophical approach to
theology based largely on the work of the great thirteenth-
century Dominican Thomas Aquinas (1225–74), the new
theology made use of the historical studies so suspicious to
many in Rome following the condemnation of Modernism
by Pope Pius X in 1907. For example, returning to the way
the liturgy was celebrated in the early church made clear that
so-called innovations such as celebrating in the vernacular
and allowing the faithful to respond to the prayers, receive
from the chalice, and take a more active role could no longer
be seen as nontraditional.

Among the *ressourcement* theologians were scholars
such as Yves Congar, Marie-Dominique Chenu, Jean Daniélou,
and Henri de Lubac in France, as well as Hans Urs von
Balthasar in Switzerland. In their work they sought to treat
God as a subject rather than an object, integrate the natural
and the supernatural, overcome the rupture between theology and life, recover the liturgical tradition of the early
church and the more active role of the laity in its celebration,

and recover the central role of scripture.[2] The Vatican's Holy Office, fearful that their scholarship was introducing dangerous innovations, had Chenu and Congar dismissed from their teaching positions, though they were ultimately to play an important role in the Council for which they had done so much to prepare the ground.

JOHN XXIII

The death of Pius XII in 1958 marked the end of an era, even if no one recognized that at the time. When the cardinals gathered in the Sistine Chapel to elect his successor, they hoped for someone to carry on his conservative legacy. But the conclave deadlocked. Finally, the cardinals turned to the seventy-seven-year-old patriarch of Venice, Cardinal Angelo Roncalli. He was clearly a compromise candidate, chosen to be a transitional pope. But John XXIII, as he chose to be known, the first pope in five hundred years to use the name John, was to bring about one of the great reform movements in the history of the church.

One of thirteen children, Roncalli came from Bergamo in northern Italy where his family worked as sharecroppers. But he was a shrewd and sophisticated churchman. Ordained in 1904, he had served as a seminary professor, as a chaplain during the First World War, and as a counselor to university students. Much of his career was spent in the papal diplomatic service, representing the Vatican in Bulgaria, Turkey, and France, making him familiar with Orthodoxy, the problems of Eastern Europe, and the theological renewal taking place in France. In 1953 he was made patriarch of Venice.

Shortly after his election to the chair of Peter, Pope John announced, on January 25, 1959, at a service to conclude the octave of prayer for Christian unity at the Basilica of Saint Paul-Outside-the-Walls, that he intended to call an ecumenical council. The result was a stunned silence from the gathered cardinals. A council was the last thing they wanted.

In the days that followed, the pope made clear his intentions. First, he wanted the Council to begin an *aggiornamento*, an Italian word difficult to translate, meaning a "renewal" or "bringing up to date" of the Catholic Church. The pope used the metaphor of opening a window to let some fresh air into the church. Second, he wanted to invite the faithful to strive for the unity for which so many were yearning. Later, he said in a radio address that he wanted the Council to "present the Church as the church of all, and *especially of the poor.*"[3] Finally, after a 1960 visit from French Jewish historian Jules Isaac, who presented a memorandum asking that the Council might review the church's relations with the Jews, Pope John gave this task to Cardinal Augustine Bea and his staff at the newly established Secretariat for Promoting Christian Unity.

While there was some resistance from the curia, the Vatican bureaucracy that assists the pope in the governance of the church, it was clear that Pope John was not to be dissuaded, hoping the Council would be a "new Pentecost" for the church. In the preparatory phase, a Theological Commission was set up, with ten sub-commissions, to prepare the *schemata* or draft documents that the bishops would discuss. Initially the sub-commissions produced seventy drafts, no doubt to bury the bishops in paper. After the first session, two of the Council fathers, Cardinal Leon Joseph Suenens of Mechelen-Brussel and Cardinal Giovanni Battista Montini of Milan, shortly to be elected Paul VI, reduced the seventy drafts to a manageable seventeen.[4] The actual documents produced by the Council numbered sixteen.

The council opened on September 11, 1962, with some

twenty-five hundred bishops and heads of the male religious orders from all over the world gathered in St. Peter's Basilica. The great nave of the church had been lined with bleachers to accommodate the bishops, who sat in full regalia, while the seven council presidents took turns presiding from a table before the altar. At the opening session, Pope John underlined his expectations for the Council with an often-cited remark: "The substance of the ancient doctrine of the deposit of faith is one thing, and the way in which it is presented is another."[5] Thus, he underlined succinctly the difference between the inner meaning of a doctrine and its historically conditioned, and therefore limited, expression.

To make clear his ecumenical intentions, Pope John took a number of highly symbolic steps. First, he invited the Orthodox and Protestant churches to send official observers to the Council. Second, he seated them in a place of honor at the head of the assembly, opposite the cardinals. Third, he established a new Vatican congregation, the Pontifical Council for Promoting Christian Unity, placing it at the service of the observers. Some of the churches were initially skeptical. Some forty observers were present when the Council opened, but by the time it closed, there were nearly one hundred. After the first two sessions, Cardinal Suenens noted that no women were present; some were added to the third session as "auditors," a number to rise to twenty-two by the time the Council concluded.

The Council met in four sessions. The bishops, with talks often prepared by their theological advisors or *periti* (among them a thirty-five year old theologian from Germany by the name of Joseph Ratzinger), critiqued the various drafts from the floor of the basilica before the bishops voted to receive or reject them. The process was serious. The initial schema of the decree on revelation passed narrowly, but, as many of the fathers judged it to be seriously flawed, Pope John withdrew it to be redrafted. Subsequently, the bishops rejected the initial draft of the Dogmatic Constitution on the Church, *De Ecclesia*, after a devastating critique from the floor.

But while the bishops debated the various documents in St. Peter's, the real business of the Council took place in the bars, restaurants, and religious houses of Rome, where the bishops, their theological advisors, non-Catholic observers, journalists, and others present in Rome gathered to review the events of the day. Life-changing friendships were formed, often across ecclesial divisions, and many of the bishops found themselves receiving an education they had never anticipated.

The pope had intended from the beginning that the Council be pastoral rather than dogmatic. It produced sixteen documents: four constitutions, nine decrees, and three declarations. While not all the documents are of equal quality, we will consider some of the more significant: Dogmatic Constitution on the Church, Dogmatic Constitution on Divine Revelation, Constitution on the Sacred Liturgy, Decree on Ecumenism, Declaration on the Relation of the Church to Non-Christian Religions, and Declaration on Religious Freedom.

THE CHURCH

At the end of the Council's first session, after the fathers had rejected the draft on the church, *De Ecclesia*, Cardinal Suenens of Malines-Brussels suggested that the Council's treatment of the church take place in two stages. First, the fathers should consider the church as the mystery of Christ living in his mystical body, thus of the interior life of the church, *ecclesia ad intra*. Second, the Council should address the relation of the church to the outside world, *ecclesia ad extra*, addressing questions of the dignity of the person, social justice, poverty, as well as war and peace. The results were two constitutions: the Dogmatic Constitution on the Church (*Lumen gentium*), and the Pastoral Constitution on the Church in the Modern World (*Gaudium et spes*).

Lumen gentium, from Christ "the light of the nations," took up how the Catholic Church understands itself. The constitution is significant for its new way of imaging the church, for its collegial theology of the episcopal office, and for its teaching on the laity. As a dogmatic constitution, *Lumen gentium* represents official teaching of the church's magisterium.

IMAGES OF THE CHURCH

Originally called *De Ecclesia* (like a thesis in a Roman seminary manual), *Lumen gentium* describes the church as a "mystery" (ch. 1), a sacrament, and a pilgrim church (ch. 7). The image of a pilgrim church, not just a pilgrim people, suggests that the church is still on its way, and thus open to change.

The opening paragraph speaks of the church as "like a sacrament or as a sign and instrument both of a very closely knit union with God and of the unity of the whole human race" (LG 1).[6] The church is thus a universal sacrament of salvation; the union of the faithful with God symbolizes or prefigures the union of all people. Gone is the "church militant" imagery suggested by the first chapter of the initial draft of the schema *De Ecclesia*. While speaking of the church as mystery, *Lumen gentium* places more emphasis on its inner life of grace than on its external, institutional structure.

Vatican II's basic image for the church is the people of God. But equally important are the metaphors of Body of Christ and temple of the Holy Spirit. Speaking of the church as the people of God (LG 2), Body of Christ (LG 7), and temple of the Holy Spirit (LG 7–8) brings out the fundamentally trinitarian structure of life in Christ and in the church. This is a long way from the *societas perfecta*, the juridical/institutional image of church that prevailed at Vatican I, a definition of the church in terms of its juridical structures of authority and governance. The image of the church as a perfect society means that the church has all it needs to achieve its ends, including the necessary freedom.[7] But to many, it suggests that there is nothing that the church has to learn from other societies, given its special nature and divine foundation. In truth, the church has borrowed from civil structures of governance in every age.

Finally, the metaphor of the church as a communion (*koinōnia*) is a powerful one. It nicely captures the way in which life in Christ and thus in the church is a participation or communion in the life of God as Father, Son, and Spirit. It also has emerged as the central metaphor for ecclesiology and ecumenism, with its vision of the church itself as a communion of churches, each a eucharistic community gathered around its bishop, or even better, the church as a communion of communions.

Thus, in shifting from a universalistic ecclesiology to an ecclesiology of communion, an ecclesiology that sees the church as a communion of churches, Vatican II effected what has been called a Copernican revolution in ecclesiology.[8] A more traditional, monarchical model of the church sees the church as a single global institution divided into administrative units, called dioceses, with all authority coming from the top down. Vatican II's ecclesiology of *communio* envisions the church as a communion of churches, providing a model for envisioning the future of a reconciled church (see Figure 1).

Figure I

MONARCHICAL MODEL

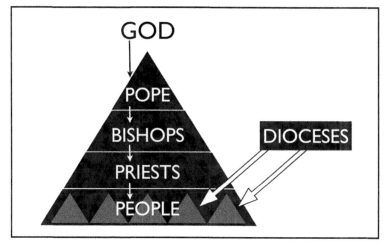

COMMUNION MODEL

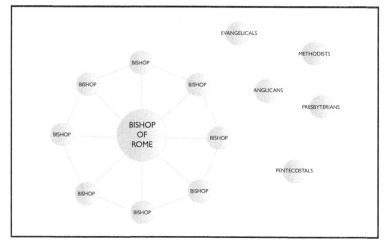

TEACHING ON BISHOPS

Perhaps the most significant and one of the most hard fought battles was the Council's teaching on the episcopal office, and specifically, on its doctrine of collegiality. During the debate on the floor of the Council, Cardinal Alfrink of Utrecht suggested that the phrase "Peter and the apostles" would be better expressed as "Peter and the *other* apostles," putting Peter back within the episcopal college. This can serve to introduce the notion of collegiality.

From the beginning of chapter 3, the Council fathers indicate that their teaching concerning bishops is a matter of doctrine (LG 18). Just as the apostles constituted a college or fixed group (LG 19), so also the bishops by divine institution succeed to the place of the apostles as pastors of the church (LG 20). Episcopal consecration confers the fullness of the sacrament of orders (LG 21, closing an old debate). Together with the Roman pontiff, the bishops have supreme and full authority over the universal church, especially at an ecumenical council (LG 21), while individual bishops are placed in charge of particular churches (LG 22). They govern their particular churches with power they possess in their own right, not by delegation from the pope.

Bishops proclaim infallibly the doctrine of Christ when they are united among themselves and with the successor of Peter (LG 25). The church's charism of infallibility is shared by the episcopal college in union with its head or can be exercised by the head of the college in the name of the bishops. It is important to note at this point how the Council reinterpreted Vatican I's teaching on primacy and infallibility by placing it in a new context.

But the constitution also states that to these definitions "the assent of the Church" can never be wanting, on account of the activity of that same Holy Spirit, by which the whole flock of Christ is preserved and progresses in unity of faith (LG 25). Thus the Council fathers made clear that bishops and pope teach what the church itself believes. In other words, the Spirit resides not just in the hierarchy but in the whole church, bishops and faithful, keeping it in the truth. The hierarchy cannot teach independently of the faith of the church, for the church is a communion of pastors and faithful, not a "top-down" institution of teachers and taught, as pre–Vatican II language suggested.

This doctrine of episcopal collegiality is one of the constitution's most important teachings. It means that the church can no longer be understood as a papal monarchy; its government is collegial, even though the pope can exercise his power personally as head or "chair" of the college, as the *Nota Praevia* emphasized. Bishops are not "branch managers" reporting to the pope, so to speak, but are themselves "vicars of Christ" (LG 27), reclaiming a title that had been reserved for the pope since the Middle Ages. In many ways the Council's teaching on the collegial nature of the episcopal office represented a retrieval of the way the church was understood and functioned in the first millennium, though now it is stated as doctrine.

The ecclesiology underlying this language is an ecclesiology of communion; again, the one church is a communion of churches. Yet Vatican II failed to resolve the tension between the universal church and the local church; in its concern to safeguard papal authority, it emphasized one-sidedly the pope's freedom to act.

THE LAITY

Also very significant was the Council's development of a theology of the laity. In the centuries since the Council of Trent, the clericalizing and centralizing of the church had reduced the laity for all intents and purposes to passive members. In a 1906 encyclical, Pope Pius X had written that "the Church is essentially an unequal society, that is, a society comprising two categories of persons, the Pastors and the flock....So distinct are these categories that with the pastoral body only rests the necessary right and authority for promoting the end of the society and directing all its members toward that end; the one duty of the multitude is to allow themselves to be led, and, like a docile flock, to follow the Pastors."[9]

A movement in the decades prior to Vatican II described the lay apostolate as "the collaboration of the laity in the apostolic tasks proper to the hierarchy," language that suggested that the mission or apostolate of the church really belonged to the hierarchy, even though Pius XII encouraged lay organizations throughout the world, "laying the groundwork for the focus on the laity that would prevail at Vatican II."[10] But the more conservative bishops were very much against the new theology of the laity that was beginning to make an impact on the Council fathers. For example, the Dominican Yves Congar had been removed from his teaching post, in part because of curial unhappiness over his book *Lay People in the Church*,[11] while the curia's Cardinal Ruffini argued that the constitution should not speak of a "mission of the laity" when in fact their mission came to them only through the hierarchy. And he objected to the idea that the charisms or spiritual gifts, so important to St. Paul (1 Cor 12—14), were still widespread in the church, arguing that today they were very rare.

Nevertheless, *Lumen gentium* took a number of significant steps to develop a theology of the laity based on their baptismal dignity. Gone was the juridical term "subjects," used in the original schema, *De Ecclesia*, to describe the laity in its chapter on obedience.[12] *Lumen gentium* used the biblical image of the people of God to describe the church (LG chap. 2), and it emphasized that the whole church, not just priests and religious, are called to holiness (LG chap. 5). This meant that the old language that described the religious life as a "state of perfection" or "higher way" was no longer appropriate. The old *Baltimore Catechism* had two pictures, one of a married couple, the other of a priest and a nun; the first said "good," the second "better."

Pneumatologically, the Council reclaimed the charismata or spiritual gifts, "both hierarchical and charismatic" (LG 4; cf. 12, 30; AA 3; PO 9), thus rejecting Cardinal Ruffini's view that the charismata were rare in the contemporary church. A theology of the charisms underlines the fundamentally pneumatological nature of the church and leads to a recovery of the Pauline vision of the church as a Spirit-led community equipped with a rich diversity of gifts and ministries. The great Dominican ecclesiologist Yves Congar saw the Council's treatment of the charisms as its most important step toward bringing into focus the role of the Holy Spirit in the church.[13] In the postconciliar church, it was to lead to the explosion of lay ministries, something completely unanticipated by the Council fathers, both in the church and in the world, where the particular vocation of the laity is to "seek the kingdom of God by engaging in temporal affairs" (LG 31).

THE CHURCH AND THE WORLD

The longest document to come out of the Council, the Pastoral Constitution on the Church in the Modern World (*Gaudium et spes*), turned the previously defensive face of the church to the world in service. Its intention was beautifully expressed in its opening sentence: "The joys and the hopes, the griefs and the anxieties of the men of this age, especially those who are poor or in any way afflicted, these

are the joys and hopes, the griefs and anxieties of the followers of Christ. Indeed, nothing genuinely human fails to
raise an echo in their hearts" (1).

The first chapter stressed the dignity of the human person
and the common good, two controlling values of Catholic
social teaching. Chapter 2 noted a growing sense of a single,
worldwide community, or what today is often referred to as
globalization. It acknowledged that the church does not
always have the solution to particular problems (GS 33) as
well as the legitimate autonomy of the sciences and human
societies, while warning against any tendency to ignore God
the Creator or to oppose science and faith (GS 36).

Speaking of the church's role in the modern world
(Chapter 4), the constitution notes that just as the church
has profited from the development of humankind and from
the evolution of social life, it has much to contribute to the
world: "It is the task of the entire People of God, especially
pastors and theologians, to hear, distinguish and interpret
the many voices of our age, and to judge them in the light of
the divine word, so that revealed truth can always be more
deeply penetrated, better understood and set forth to greater
advantage" (GS 44).

In Part 2, the constitution addresses "some problems of
special urgency." It stresses the dignity of marriage and the
family (GS 47). It notes the tension that often exists between
culture and Christian thought, calling on theologians to
work to find ways to communicate more suitably the
church's teaching, drawing on the secular sciences, observing
that if they are to fulfill their functions, "let it be recognized
that all the faithful, whether clerics or laity, possess a lawful
freedom of inquiry, freedom of thought," and it expressed
the hope that many of the laity would receive a formation in
the "sacred sciences," that is, theology (GS 62).

In the area of economic and social life, it argues that economic production is not just for more profit; it is meant to be at the service of humanity, noting with a quotation from the church fathers, "Feed the man dying of hunger, because if you have not fed him, you have killed him," that in extreme necessity those in need are entitled to take what they need from the riches of others (GS 69). In regard to the life of the political community, it defends the rights of freedom of assembly, expression, religion, participation in political life, and of minorities (GS 73).

The final section, on fostering peace and a community of nations, speaks against the arms race, noting its devastating effect on the poor and the threat it poses to all humanity (GS 81). It calls for serious steps toward disarmament and for some kind of international community, for greater coopera-tion among nations, aid and assistance to developing coun-tries, and a brotherhood that embraces all.

DIVINE REVELATION

The Council's Dogmatic Constitution on Divine Reve-lation (*Dei verbum*) moved dramatically beyond the Catholic Church's post-Reformation hesitancy about Scripture to place it again at the center of the church's life. Reacting to the Reformation proclamation of *sola Scriptura*, Scripture alone, the Catholic Church had been reluctant to encourage the faithful to read the Bible, less they fall into what it considered the Protestant error of "private interpretation." As a result, generations of Catholics grew up reading carefully prepared books of Bible stories but not the Bible itself. Now the Council stressed that Sacred Scripture should be venerated in the church the same as the Body of Christ in the Eucharist (DV 21). It should be the soul of theology and nourish the church's preaching, catechesis, and Christian instruction, especially in the liturgical homily (DV 24).

Theologically, the Council moved Catholic thinking beyond a propositional model of revelation, evident in Trent speaking of the "truths and rules" of the gospel. Revelation was not abstract truths or confessional formulas, but personal, God's self-communication in history, reaching its full manifestation in the man Jesus, the Word become flesh, and offering men and women a share in God's own divine nature through the Spirit (DV 2). Thus, revelation is not identified with either text or tradition; it is trinitarian in form, historical in mediation, and christological in realization.

Since revelation comes to us in the words of human beings, biblical interpreters need to pay attention to the historical circumstances in which the biblical authors wrote and the literary forms they employed, thus stressing the importance of the historical-critical method of biblical interpretation. At the same time, Scripture is always read within the living tradition of the church, under the guidance of the magisterium (DV 12). Thus, *Dei verbum* ended the Catholic Church's benign neglect of Scripture; its impact on Catholic theology and Catholic life is inestimable.

LITURGY

No doubt the document that had the most impact on Catholics was the Constitution on the Sacred Liturgy (*Sacrosanctum concilium*). Building on the liturgical movement that preceded the Council, the constitution sought to renew the liturgical life of the church, that is, its worship and sacraments. Its first principle was full and active participation, with the word *participation* appearing sixteen times. Simply stated, "Mother Church earnestly desires that all the faithful should be led to that fully conscious, and active participation in liturgical celebrations which is demanded by the very nature of the liturgy" (SC 14). "To promote active participation, the people should be encouraged to take part by means of acclamations, responses, psalmody, antiphons, and songs, as well as by actions, gestures, and bodily attitudes. And at the proper times all should observe a reverent silence" (SC 3).

Second, the constitution emphasized the essentially communal nature of the liturgy: "Liturgical services are not private functions, but are celebrations of the Church, which is the 'sacrament of unity'" (SC 26); in other words, the whole assembly celebrates, not just the priest, who is more properly referred to as the presider. The postconciliar liturgies would see a diversity of liturgical ministries beyond that of the priest.

Third, the constitution called for a simplification of the rites, which "should be distinguished by a noble simplicity; they should be short, clear, and unencumbered by useless repetitions; they should be within the people's powers of comprehension, and normally should not require much explanation" (SC 34). This led to a revision of the liturgy of the Mass and the sacraments as well as the breviary, now known as the *Prayer of Christians*.

Finally, the constitution moved cautiously in the direction of greater inculturation of the liturgy. It extended the use of vernacular language in the Mass and the sacraments and made provision "for legitimate variations and adaptations to different groups, regions, and peoples, especially in mission lands" when revising liturgical books (SC 38).

The changes in the liturgy within a few years of the council were dramatic. Episcopal conferences moved to translate the liturgy into the vernacular; the rites were revised, new translations and lectionaries were provided, and everywhere the faithful began to take a more active role in the celebration.

ECUMENISM

One of the Council's most significant reforms was to officially commit the Roman Catholic Church to the ecumenical movement. Although the Catholic Church had continued to recognize the Orthodox churches as churches after the division between East and West in 1054, in the twentieth century its ecclesial language had become increasingly exclusive. Pope Pius XI stated that no one could be in the one church of Christ without submission to the pope,[14] and Pius XII identified the mystical body of Christ with the Roman Catholic Church in his 1943 encyclical *Mystici corporis* (no. 13), implying that only Catholics are members of the body of Christ.[15] In his 1950 encyclical *Humani generis*, he stated again that Catholics must hold that the mystical body of Christ and the Roman Catholic Church are one and the same thing.[16] This same exclusive language appeared in the first draft of the schema *De Ecclesia*: "The Roman Catholic Church is the Mystical Body of Christ...and only the one that is Roman Catholic has the right to be called church."[17]

During the debates at Vatican II's first session, a number of fathers criticized this language. *Lumen gentium*, the document ultimately approved by the fathers in 1964, took a number of steps to reformulate the Catholic understanding of the relation of the Catholic Church to other Christian communities. First, the original schema's exclusive identification of the mystical body of Christ with the Catholic Church was qualified in what became the final 1964 text, which reads: "This Church constituted and organized in the world as a society, subsists in the Catholic Church, which is governed by the successor of Peter and by the Bishops in communion with him" (LG 8).

Second, the constitution added that "many elements of sanctification and of truth are found outside of its visible structure. These elements, as gifts belonging to the Church of Christ, are forces impelling toward catholic unity" (LG 8). Calling attention to these "elements of sanctification" and changing "is" to "subsists in" was extremely significant, as it signified that the Roman Catholic Church was no longer claiming an exclusive identity or strict equation between the church of Christ and itself, or more positively, it suggested that the church extends in some way beyond the boundaries of the Catholic Church.[18]

The Decree on Ecumenism (*Unitatis redintegratio*) laid out the principles for Catholic participation in ecumenism. Most important, it stated that "there can be no ecumenism worthy of the name without interior conversion" (UR 7) and begged pardon for the sins of Catholics against unity. Many of us have forgotten, or are too young to know, how moved representatives of the other churches were by this gracious move by the fathers of the Council. The decree taught that all those properly baptized are already in a real, though imperfect communion with the Catholic Church (UR 3), emphasizing that because of the divisions, the Catholic Church cannot realize the fullness of catholicity proper to it (UR 4).

The Decree on Ecumenism encouraged common prayer with other Christians, though it argued that witness to the lack of unity generally forbids common worship (*communicatio in sacris*), leaving individual cases up to local bishops' conferences or the Holy See (UR 8). It also observed that there is a "hierarchy of truths" (UR 11). It distinguished between the divisions in the East, the Orthodox Churches recognized by the Council as possessing true sacraments and by apostolic succession, the priesthood (UR 15), and those in the West, those "ecclesial communities" issuing from the sixteenth-century Reformation, which, in the opinion of the Council fathers because of the absence (*defectus*) of the sacrament of orders, "have not retained the proper reality of the eucharistic mystery in its fullness." Notice that the decree does not say that they do not have the Eucharist, only that something is missing, recommending dialogue on these and other issues that continue to divide the churches (UR 22).

VIEW OF NON-CHRISTIANS

The Council discussed other Christians in *Lumen gentium* and again in *Nostra aetate*, the Declaration on the Relationship of the Church to Non-Christian Religions. *Lumen gentium* addresses the relationship of those "who have not yet accepted the Gospel" but are related to the people of God in various ways.

First, *Lumen gentium* speaks of the consideration to the Jewish people when treating the relationship of the other religions to the people of God and echoes Paul's teaching that they are a people, "beloved, for the sake of their ancestors; for the gifts and the calling of God are irrevocable" (LG 16; cf. Rom 11:28–29). This was echoed by *Nostra aetate*, which rejected all forms of anti-Semitism and emphasized that responsibility for the death of Jesus could not be placed on all the Jews at the time of his passion, nor on the Jews today (NA 4). In doing this, the council moved beyond the "supercessionist" or replacement theology that had long been popular, suggesting that God's covenant relationship with the Jewish people no longer applied because of their failure to recognize Jesus. "Although the Church is the new people of God, the Jews should not be presented as rejected or accursed by God, as if this followed from the Holy Scriptures" (NA 4). Thus, the Council rejected the anti-Judaism responsible for so much anti-Semitism as well as the charge of "deicide," making possible the new relationship with the Jewish people, which developed in the postconciliar years.[19]

In regard to Muslims, the Council taught that "they profess to hold the faith of Abraham, and together with us they adore the one, merciful God" (LG 16).

Finally, *Lumen gentium* addresses those who belong to other world religions or to no religion at all:

> Those also can attain to salvation who through no fault of their own do not know the Gospel of Christ or His Church, yet sincerely seek God and moved by grace strive by their deeds to do His will as it is known to them through the dictates of conscience. Nor does Divine Providence deny the helps necessary for salvation to those who, without blame on their part, have not yet arrived at an explicit knowledge of God and with His grace strive to live a good life. (LG 16)

Here the Council clearly recognizes the possibility of salvation for those who have neither been baptized nor evangelized. It does not, as is sometimes alleged, move to a doctrine of universal salvation, for it acknowledges the power of sin or what it refers to as the deceptions of the "Evil One." Nevertheless, in its teaching on God's universal salvific will and the presence of grace in those who have not been evangelized, the Council has moved Catholic teaching significantly forward. Francis Sullivan speaks of this as "a decisive change in Catholic thinking about the salvation of those 'outside.'"[20]

Speaking of the great religions of the world, the Council affirmed that "the Catholic Church rejects nothing that is true and holy in these religions. She regards with sincere reverence those ways of conduct and of life, those precepts and teachings which, though differing in many aspects from the ones she holds and sets forth, nonetheless often reflect a ray of that Truth which enlightens all men" (NA 2). In other words, God's Spirit is in some mysterious way at work in these religions also, something that was acknowledged by Pope John Paul II.

RELIGIOUS LIBERTY

The greatest battle at the Council, bitterly contested by those who followed the traditional argument that "error has no rights," was over religious freedom. The more conservative members of the Council wanted the church to continue to maintain that in predominantly Catholic countries (like Spain or those in Latin America), the church should in principle be able to prohibit the practice or spread of religions it considers false. Other faiths, including other Christian faiths, might be tolerated for political reasons, but they had no intrinsic right to equality of treatment.

But here again, the Council moved Catholic teaching forward. Its Declaration on Religious Freedom (*Dignitatis humanae*) taught that the human person has a right to religious freedom, rooted in the very dignity of the human person, which is known through the revealed word of God and, therefore, should be recognized by constitutional law whereby society is governed. Thus, it becomes a civil right (DH 2). Religious bodies, a requirement of the social nature of human beings, "have the right not to be hindered in their public teaching and witness to their faith, whether by the spoken or by the written word" (DH 4).

CONCLUSION

While Pope John XXIII and many members of the curia thought that the Second Vatican Council could finish its work in the course of a year, it actually took four years to bring it to a conclusion. That a global institution as old and as complex as the Roman Catholic Church could take a critical look at itself, and do it successfully, was a surprise to many. *Lumen gentium*, in developing a collegial theology of the episcopal office, pointed the way to the reform of authority in the church, even if its actual reception in the life of the church was by no means immediate. The theology of the laity developed by the Council was to result in the totally unexpected explosion of lay ministries in the postconciliar period. The Council committed the Catholic Church, somewhat late, to the ecumenical movement, which was to give it new energy, while *Nostra aetate* was to make possible the dialogue among different religions, so important today in the twenty-first century.

The biggest change for most Catholics came from *Sacrosanctum concilium*, the Constitution on the Sacred Liturgy. Within a very few years, most Catholic churches were celebrating the liturgy in the vernacular, while the rites for the sacraments and the Mass itself were revised and laymen and laywomen began to take new and active roles in the celebration. The Pastoral Constitution on the Church in the Modern World (*Gaudium et spes*) was to place issues of social justice and concern for the poor at the center of the church's concerns and lead to new movements and theologies of liberation.

Not all were comfortable with *Gaudium et spes*, finding it too optimistic. Drafted largely by some of the French and Belgian bishops and theologians, the pastoral constitution emphasized the concept of dialogue, seeing the relationship between the church and world as a "colloquium" or conversation, as though both could enter into dialogue as equals.

Others, among them Joseph Ratzinger and Karl Rahner, believed that its approach ignored the reality of sin in the world. Ratzinger questioned its pretheological concept of world, its emphasis on dialogue, and the "astonishing optimism" it displayed.[21] Rahner found its undertone "too euphoric in its evaluation of humanity and the human condition," insisting that all human endeavors often wind up in blind alleys, including those of the church, which he refers to as a "Church of sinners."[22] Others noted that it placed more emphasis on the mediating function of the church than on Jesus and his proclamation of the kingdom of God.

But the Council succeeded beyond anyone's expectations in bringing the Catholic Church into the modern world. In spite of the obvious changes in the liturgy and new attitudes toward the religious "other," one could argue that its most profound impact on the life of the church is only beginning to be felt. In the first year of his pontificate, Pope Francis addressed this issue. He asked if Catholics have opened themselves to "that continuity of the church's growth" that the Council signified. The answer, he said, is "no." Catholics seemed willing to celebrate the fiftieth anniversary of the Council's opening in 1962, he said, but they want to do so by "building a monument" rather than by changing anything.[23] So the work of the Council is still unfinished.

NOTES

1. John W. O'Malley, *Tradition and Transition: Historical Perspectives on Vatican II* (Wilmington, DE: Michael Glazier, 1988), 17.

2. See Hans Boersma, *Nouvelle Théologie and Sacramental Ontology: A Return to Mystery* (Oxford: Oxford University Press, 2009).

3. Peter Hebblethwaite, "John XXIII," in *Modern Catholicism: Vatican II and After,* ed. Adrian Hastings (New York: Oxford University Press, 1991), 30.

4. Peter Hebblethwaite, *Paul VI: The First Modern Pope* (New York: Paulist, 1993), 314.

5. Text in Walter M. Abbott, ed., *The Documents of Vatican II* (New York: Herder & Herder, 1966), 715.

6. From this point, citations from the documents of the Council are taken from the Vatican website.

7. Yves Congar, "Moving towards a Pilgrim Church," in *Vatican II Revisited by Those Who Were There*, ed. Alberic Stacpoole (Minneapolis, MN: Winston Press, 1986), 138.

8. Joseph A. Komonchak, "The Local Church and the Church Catholic: The Contemporary Theological Problematic," *The Jurist* 52 (1952): 432.

9. Pope Pius X, *Vehementor nos*, no. 8; ET, *The Papal Encyclicals*, vol. 3, ed. Claudia Carlen (New York: McGrath, 1981): 47–48.

10. John W. O'Malley, *What Happened at Vatican II* (Cambridge, MA: Harvard University Press, 2008), 81.

11. Yves Congar, *Lay People in the Church; A Study for a Theology of the Laity* (Westminster, MD: Newman Press, 1957).

12. O'Malley, *What Happened at Vatican II*, 174.

13. Yves Congar, *I Believe in the Holy Spirit* (New York: Crossroad, 1983), 1:170.

14. *AAS* 20 (1928), 15

15. The same teaching appears in Pius XII's 1950 encyclical *Humani generis* (27).

16. See Francis A. Sullivan, *The Church We Believe In: One, Holy, Catholic, and Apostolic* (New York: Paulist Press, 1988), 16; text in *AAS* 42 (1950), 571.

17. *Acta Synodalia Concilii Vaticani II* (Vatican City, 1970ff.), I/4, 15, cited in Sullivan, *The Church We Believe In*, 23.

18. Cf. Pope John Paul II, *Ut Unum Sint*, no. 11: "To the extent that these elements are found in other Christian Communities, the one Church of Christ is effectively present in them."

19. For the background to the Council's teaching on the Jews, see John Connelly, *From Enemy to Brother: The Revolution in*

Catholic Teaching on the Jews 1933–1965 (Cambridge, MA: Harvard University Press, 2012).

20. Francis A. Sullivan, *Salvation outside the Church? Tracing the History of the Catholic Response* (New York: Paulist Press, 1992), 160.

21. See Joseph Ratzinger, *Principles of Catholic Theology* (San Francisco: Ignatius Press, 1987), 380.

22. Karl Rahner, *Theological Investigations*, vol. 22 (New York: Crossroad, 1991), 158.

23. Catholic News Service, "Pope Francis Says Catholics Still Need to Enact the Teachings of Vatican II" (April 16, 2013); http://www.catholicnews.com/data/stories/cns/1301701.htm.

CHAPTER 8

BENEDICT
AND FRANCIS

As the Roman Catholic Church moved into the twenty-first century, the long pontificate of Pope John Paul II, the first non-Italian pope since the sixteenth century, came to an end with his death in 2005. His remarkable pontificate had lasted almost twenty-seven years. He had played a significant role in the collapse of the communist governments across Eastern Europe; celebrated the new millennium with a great Jubilee Year, inviting the church to an examination of conscience and purification of memory; and twice called representatives of the world's religions together for prayer and a renunciation of violence at Assisi, first in 1986 and again after 9/11. In doing so, he showed the possibility for church leadership on a global scale.

While most papal observers did not expect German Cardinal Joseph Ratzinger, who had served Pope John Paul for twenty-four years as prefect of the Vatican's powerful Congregation for the Doctrine of the Faith, to succeed him; he was elected on April 19 as Pope Benedict XVI after just four ballots. When Benedict shocked many by retiring eight years later, in 2013, another non-Italian was elected, this time an Argentinian, Cardinal Jorge Mario Bergoglio, Archbishop of Buenos Aires. Before looking at the Catholic Church today, we need to review the work of these two popes.

POPE BENEDICT XVI

Joseph Ratzinger was born in the Bavarian village of Marktl am Inn on April 16, 1927, and baptized that same day. He grew up during the Second World War, serving in an anti-aircraft battery and later in an army service battalion. After a few months as a prisoner of war, he resumed his studies for the priesthood and for a doctorate in theology. He was ordained on June 29, 1951.

Brought to the Second Vatican Council by Cardinal Joseph Frings, Archbishop of Cologne, the young theologian was just thirty-five years old when the Council began in 1962. But he was to play a role in the development of some of the Council's most important documents, among them the Dogmatic Constitution on Divine Revelation (*Dei Verbum*), the Dogmatic Constitution on the Church (*Lumen gentium*), the Pastoral Constitution on the Church in the Modern World (*Gaudium et spes*), and the Decree on the Mission Activity of the Church (*Ad gentes*).[1] As prefect of the Congregation for the Doctrine of the Faith, and then as pope, he exercised a care for the integrity of Catholic doctrine in an era of considerable pluralism, both in theology and in the postconciliar dialogue with other religious traditions.

When he was elected to the chair of Peter, Ratzinger had an international reputation as a theologian, with over one hundred books and four times as many articles. His astonishing range of interests extends from dogmatic theology to liturgy, culture and the arts, politics, ecumenism, and non-Christian religions. His *Introduction to Christianity*,[2] one of his most successful books, has been translated into at least nineteen languages, including Arabic and Chinese, while his three-volume work on Christology, *Jesus of Nazareth*, is a modern classic.

THEOLOGICAL ANTHROPOLOGY

At the heart of Pope Benedict's thought is his theological anthropology, a theology of the human person created in the image and likeness of God, who in the divine inner life is defined in terms of relations. This anthropology, grounded in the Fatherhood of God and Christ's solidarity with all people, in turn underlines a theology of universal brotherhood as the task of the church. Like his teacher Augustine, Benedict has always stressed the difference between knowledge (*scientia*) and wisdom (*sapientia*), insisting that one has to love the truth in order to know it, and he has always seen beauty as a path to the Divine. In *Jesus of Nazareth*, he comments that the organ for seeing God is the heart.[3]

Another concern of Benedict is the integral relationship between faith and reason. In *Truth and Tolerance*, he wrote: "Reason needs to listen to the great religious traditions if it does not wish to become deaf, blind, and mute concerning the most essential elements of human existence."[4] At the same time faith needs reason if it is not to fall into some kind of fundamentalism. He has long criticized modern, secular reason, which, in privileging a scientific model of knowing cut off from its Christian roots, has become pathological in assuming autonomy without reference to the transcendent. In the final analysis, only conscience, properly understood, can preserve people from injustice; no institution can do this by itself.

ECCLESIOLOGY

Benedict's ecclesiology is centered on the church's eucharistic foundation and its nature as a communion (*communio*). With appeals to Paul in 1 Corinthians 10:16–17, he argues that we become the one Body of Christ by sharing in the Eucharist: "The Church is the cerebration of the Eucharist: The Eucharist is the Church; they do not simply stand side by side; they are one and the same."[5] From this flows his second theme, the church as a communion. The church is not a federation of communities, still less of denominations, but the one church existing in many local churches, in communion with each other and with the bishop of Rome.

His reflections on the Council, published shortly after it concluded, showed him to be on the side of reform. He pointed to papal centralism as an obvious problem and an obstacle for ecumenism; he also called for a reform of the Roman Curia, a quiet review of priestly celibacy, and a strong synod of bishops.[6] Later he moved in a different direction. Concerned about what he saw as the negative side of the liturgical renewal, he began what has been described as a reform of the reform. After reading an article by Henri de Lubac, he rethought his position on the theological status of episcopal conferences, seeing them now as products of ecclesiastical rather than divine law,[7] and he warned about their growing bureaucratic structures. As prefect of the Congregation for the Doctrine of the Faith (CDF) and under the direction of Pope John Paul II, he issued a number of documents to strengthen and extend the authority of the magisterium.

In terms of ecumenism, he played a role in the acceptance of the 1998 Lutheran-Catholic Joint Declaration on the Doctrine of Justification by the Catholic Church and the Lutheran World Federation, while relations between the Catholic Church and the Orthodox churches, particularly the Russian Orthodox Church, warmed considerably during his pontificate. More controversial was the CDF's 2000 declaration *Dominus Iesus* and his *Anglicanorum coetibus*, establishing a Personal Ordinariate for disaffected Anglicans, though his initiative has been welcomed by those among them wanting to enter into full communion with the Catholic Church.

POLITICAL PHILOSOPHY

Though widely acclaimed for his properly theological writings, the depth of Ratzinger/Benedict's work in the area of political philosophy is less well known. As political scientist and philosopher Thomas Rourke notes, Benedict shows far more depth in this area "than one usually finds in the writings of political scientists and other social writers," a depth he attributes to his richer understanding of historical trends and developments in Western thought.[8] After 9/11 he took part in a public dialogue with Jürgen Habermas of the neo-Marxist Frankfurt School on the question of the inability of the state to justify the very values it seeks to promote, since it is not itself the source of truth or morality, part of a larger dialogue between believers (*credenti*) and secular (*laici*) voices. At the beginning of his papacy, he dared to raise the difficult question of religion and violence in his much misunderstood lecture at Regensburg (2006). Later, in *Spe salvi*, Benedict appealed to Theodor Adorno, also of the Frankfurt School, to critique a naive faith in technological progress that Adorno once described as "progress from the sling to the atom bomb."

At the same time, Benedict has long been against any kind of political theology, seeing in modern attempts to find salvation through political activity or technological progress a secularization of Christian hope. From the time of his *Habilitationsschrift* on Bonaventure's theology of history, he has contested any effort to "immanentize" the eschaton, to use a term of Eric Vögelin,[9] that is, to make it something *within* history rather than *beyond* it. Similarly, he resists efforts to separate the kingdom of God from Christ or the church.[10] Such efforts would make the mission of the church primarily social, emptying theology of its transcendent dimension, ignoring Jesus as God's presence active in history in a new way, and turning Christianity into an ideology. Bringing the eschaton into time, such as in Marxism, also fails to recognize that the goal or end of history has been already revealed in the person of Jesus "who is recognized as the last man (the second Adam), that is as the long-awaited manifestation of what is truly human and the definitive revelation to man of his hidden nature."[11] He took up these themes again in his encyclical *Spe salvi*.

AFFIRMATIVE ORTHODOXY

From the beginning of his pontificate, Pope Benedict sought to counter the popular view that Christianity is nothing more than a collection of rules or prohibitions. American journalist John L. Allen, a longtime Vatican watcher, characterizes his style as one of "affirmative orthodoxy," a concern to present Christianity in a positive light:

> By "affirmative orthodoxy," I mean a tenacious defense of the core elements of classic Catholic doctrine, but presented in a relentlessly positive key. Benedict appears convinced that the gap between the faith and contemporary secular culture, which Paul VI called "the drama of our time," has its roots in Europe dating from the Reformation, the Wars of Religion, and the Enlightenment, with a resulting tendency to see Christianity as a largely negative system of prohibitions and controls. In effect, Benedict's project is to reintroduce Christianity from the ground up, in terms of what it's for rather than what it's against.[12]

Even more important, his deepest conviction is that being a Christian is the result of entering into a relationship with the person of Jesus, a theme he reiterated in his first encyclical, *Deus caritas est* (no. 1). The encyclical presents a personal God who is love itself and who loves creation and human beings passionately. This concern was behind his declaring 2012 a Year of Faith, beginning on October 11, 2012, the fiftieth anniversary of the opening of the Second Vatican Council, and calling representatives of the worldwide episcopacy to Rome for a Synod on the New Evangelization. From the beginning of his papacy, he has been concerned to reassert a strong Christian identity in the face of the secularism of Europe. He fears that Europe is losing its soul, or in the words of Benedict scholar James Corkery, that it suffers from "a strange lack of confidence both about its past and about its future."[13] With negative birth rates and the church's continued loss of members, the only religion that seems to be growing in Europe is Islam.

Pope John Paul II did more to advance interreligious dialogue than any pope in history. In his encyclical *Redemptoris missio*, he acknowledged the Spirit's presence outside of Christianity; he affirmed that the "Spirit's presence and activity affect not only the individuals but also society and history, peoples, cultures and religions" (no. 28), which is to say that the spirit is mysteriously present in other religions and cultures, even if Jesus remains the one savior of all, and so the church must continue to evangelize. Though he did not call these religions mediations of saving grace in their own right, he spoke of "participated forms of mediation of different kinds and degrees," acquiring meaning from Christ, the one mediator between God and humankind (no. 5). The magisterium has not yet spoken authoritatively on the possibility of other religions mediating salvation. But the Catholic Church's ability to recognize that non-Christians are not excluded from God's salvific grace makes it far more able to enter into dialogue with the great world religions and thus with all the world's peoples.

Pope Benedict is much more cautious in speaking of salvific grace or the Spirit's presence in other religions. *Dominus Iesus*, written under his prefecture of the CDF, spoke of those in other religions as capable of receiving divine grace but said, "*objectively speaking* they are in a gravely deficient situation in comparison with those who, in the Church, have the fullness of the means of salvation" (no. 22).

CLERGY ABUSE SCANDAL

Perhaps one of the greatest challenges Benedict faced as pope was the continuing fallout from the scandal of the sexual abuse of children by clergy, especially as it became evident that this was not just an "American problem" but one that affected many countries in Europe as well. While still head of the CDF, he played an important role in centralizing the way the Vatican dealt with accusations of sexual abuse by clerics. In 2001 he ordered that all cases be reported to the CDF, implemented in John Paul's The Norms of the Motu Proprio (*Sacramentorum Sanctitatis Tutela*). According to Archbishop Vincent Nichols of Westminster, he helped bring about changes in church law, among them "the inclusion in canon law of Internet offenses against children, the extension of child abuse offenses to include the sexual abuse of all under 18, the case by case waiving of the statute of limitations and the establishment of a fast-track dismissal from the clerical state for offenders."[14]

Furthermore, as prefect of the CDF, he reviewed all these cases,[15] which provided him with a long and painful education. Shortly after becoming pope, he ordered the founder of the Legionaries of Christ, Father Marcial Maciel Degollado, against whom at least nine former seminarians had brought allegations of abuse and who it was later learned had fathered three children, to cease all public ministry and retire to a life of prayer and penance. Though these allegations went back to at least the mid-nineties, Maciel had been repeatedly praised by Pope John Paul. In 2004 Ratzinger initiated an investigation of the charges on his own authority.

Finally, during his visit to the United States in 2008, he met with five men and women who had been abused by members of the clergy, praying with them and grasping their hands. All accounts described the meeting as very moving. He raised the scandal of sexual abuse by clergy at least five times, acknowledging to the bishops that it had been "sometimes very badly handled."[16] He also met with victims of sexual abuse in Australia and on the island of Malta. In his letter to the Catholics of Ireland, he expressed his willingness to meet with some of the victims there.

BENEDICT'S LEGACY

The church Benedict leaves behind will treasure the legacy of his teaching, expressed in so many written works. But it also needs new energy, strong leadership, and a new vision, especially in the West, which is restless with more than a lack of faith. There are new questions that haven't really been discussed; they need to be addressed, as Benedict suggested in announcing his retirement, bringing the riches of the tradition, the wisdom of the church's pastors, and the scholarship of its theologians to bear.

The sudden news of his resignation on February 11, 2013, should not have taken so many by surprise. He had several times raised the possibility of a pope resigning, telling journalist Peter Seewald in 2010 that "if a pope clearly realizes that he is no longer physically, psychologically, and spiritually capable of handling the duties of office, then he has a right and, under some circumstances, also an obligation to resign."[17] Still, the news when it came was something of a bombshell.

Clearly he did it for the good of the church, and his freedom to give up his office was a sign of this remarkable man's humility and spiritual freedom. The office was never about him. Indeed, for this quiet but gracious scholar, it must have been a considerable burden. And with his intelligence, he no doubt recognized that the church needed the strong leadership that he was no longer able to provide. He had watched at close hand the once vital Pope John Paul II's long descent into illness and infirmity. And as his own energies continued to diminish, the possibility of retirement could not have been far from his mind.

It is also true that management was not a strong suit for this scholar-pope. In his last year, there had been continuing rumors that the Vatican was lacking clear leadership. Furthermore, the church was facing new challenges and questions. As he said in his retirement statement, "In today's world, subject to so many rapid changes and shaken by questions of deep relevance for the life of faith, in order to govern the bark of Saint Peter and proclaim the Gospel, both strength of mind and body are necessary, strength which in the last few months, has deteriorated in me to the extent that I have had to recognize my incapacity to adequately fulfill the ministry entrusted to me." And so with remarkable courage, Pope Benedict, often stereotyped as a conservative, took the unprecedented step of retiring, the first pope in six hundred years to do so. His resignation, an example for his successors, will stand as an important part of his legacy.

POPE FRANCIS

It could be argued that, during his final years, Pope Benedict had stacked the Sacred College of Cardinals in favor of a European. Of the 115 cardinal electors, 78 came from Europe or North America, only 39 from the rest of the world. But Cardinal Jorge Mario Bergoglio of Buenos Aires had caught the attention of many of the cardinals, and once the conclave began, after only five ballots, they placed him on the chair of Peter. He is the first pope from the Southern hemisphere, where two-thirds of the world's Catholics live today, the first from the Americas, and the first Jesuit!

The cardinal from Buenos Aires came to the conclave with little baggage and a round-trip ticket. He checked into a modest hotel for clergy in a former Jesuit college, a considerable way from the Vatican. While he had the support of a number of cardinals from Latin America, Africa, and Asia who viewed him as an outsider, few mentioned him as an obvious candidate. Many considered him too old. But on March 7, after he took his turn addressing the congregation in a four-minute talk, using notes written in his tiny script on a piece of white paper, the others took a new look at him.

He warned that the leaders of the church had become too focused on its inner life. It was navel gazing, too self-referential. "When the church is self-referential," he said, "inadvertently, she believes she has her own light; she ceases to be the *mysterium lunae* and gives way to that very serious evil, spiritual worldliness." Roman Catholicism, he said, needed to shift its focus outward, to the world beyond Vatican City walls, to the outside. The new pope "must be a man who, from the contemplation and adoration of Jesus Christ, helps the church to go out to the existential peripheries that helps her to be the fruitful mother, who gains life from the sweet and comforting joy of evangelizing."[18]

Born in Buenos Aires in 1936 of Italian parents who had fled Italy in 1929 after Mussolini came to power, Bergoglio grew up speaking both Spanish and Italian. Two of his great loves were soccer and the tango. He thought about the priesthood early in his life, but he really discovered his vocation after being overwhelmed by an experience of God's mercy after going to confession when he was seventeen. He entered the Society of Jesus in 1958 at the age of twenty-two.

Named archbishop of Buenos Aires in 1998 and cardinal in 2001, he was the runner up to Joseph Ratzinger at the 2005 conclave, so he was certainly well known to the cardinal electors. He was then sixty-eight years old. When Benedict resigned eight years later, he was seventy-six, too old to be named among the *papable*. But he was widely known and respected. In Latin America, he is clearly a leader. He addressed the sex-abuse scandal in his book *On Heaven and Earth*, saying: "We must never turn a blind eye....I do not believe in taking positions that uphold a certain corporate spirit to avoid damaging the image of the institution. That solution was proposed once in the United States: they proposed switching the priests to a different parish. It is a stupid idea; that way, the priest just takes the problem with him wherever he goes."[19]

THE CONCLAVE OF 2013

What were the needs the cardinals were most concerned about at the conclave? In the first place was the reform of the Roman Curia. While this has often been framed in terms of the reform of the Vatican bank, for many of the cardinals it also means returning to a more collegial style of governance; specifically, this means giving the bishops through their episcopal conferences more authority, a greater share in the government of the church, and improved relations between the center and the periphery, in other words, a less centralized administration. Other issues on the cardinals' agenda included the sex-abuse crisis, the needs of the global church, and the new evangelization. The cardinals would continue to be concerned about how to preach the gospel and call back to the practice of the faith the many who in our secularized western society had strayed from it.

A Different Style

Interviews with Cardinal Bergoglio, which surfaced immediately after his election, suggested that his personal style and theological vision were quite different from those of his predecessors. His way of life is simple, taking the bus to work, cooking his own meals, and living in a simple apartment rather than the episcopal palace. Shortly after his election, he announced that he would not live in the papal apartments but rather in the Domus Sanctae Marthae, the Vatican guesthouse built in 1996 under Pope John Paul II and home for some of the priests and bishops who work in the Vatican. He would live there with the other residents and say his morning Mass there. Shortly after his election, Francis telephoned the Jesuit father general, as he likes to make his own phone calls. The receptionist at the curia answered the phone, and when Francis said, "This is Papa Francesco," the receptionist said, "Sure you are." It took a while to convince him that it was indeed the holy father calling.

Pope Francis's speech is not about theologies, but it is rich in images from the Bible or the fathers of the church. His style is personal, direct, and often humorous. For example, he has expressed a healthy skepticism about claims of healings, revelations, and visions, saying that God is not like Federal Express, sending us messages all the time. The real tests of supernatural phenomena, he says are "simplicity, humility and the absence of a spectacle"—otherwise, he said, we may be dealing with a "business" rather than the presence of the Divine. But his formal addresses are theologically sophisticated.

THE POPE'S VISION

Pope Francis will certainly show himself to be an advocate for the poor. He has lived and worked among them in Buenos Aires, a city that has great disparities between the very wealthy and the very poor. Perhaps one-third of its residents live below the poverty line. It is a megacity, with close to three million in the city itself and some thirteen million in the metropolitan area. He told EWTN in 2012 that people in developed countries care more for their dogs than for their children and spend untold amounts of money on cosmetics. He has washed and kissed the feet of those addicted to drugs and afflicted with AIDS.

In his sermons from his pulpit in Buenos Aires, speaking on behalf of trafficked women, abused children, and those victimized by the drug trade, he sounds like an Old Testament prophet, or perhaps like El Salvador's Oscar Romero. Listen to just a few of his words:

> "In this city there are many slaves!...I repeat it...sweatshops...trafficking of girls in prostitution. The night before last, a poor girl was taken out of a brothel and had to be hospitalized in intensive care at one of our hospitals because to break her will they gave her psychotropics, and she entered a coma.... This city makes these great mafia lords very elegant! They may eat in Puerto Madero restaurants, but their money is stained with blood...They are the enslavers!"[20]

In an interview published shortly after his election, he referred to the Aparecida Conference, the fifth General Conference of the Latin American Bishops, as "an act of the Magisterium of the Latin American Church."[21] Interesting language, after Pope Benedict had made clear that episcopal conferences have no magisterial authority unless unanimous or approved by Rome. The Aparecida document did not originate from prepared texts but from an open dialogue. He said it "came from below, from the People of God," using a term that has been rarely used in recent Roman documents. Bergoglio himself played a major role in preparing the final document.

He called the Aparecida document the *Evangelii nuntiandi* of Latin America, referring to what is recognized as Pope Paul VI's finest apostolic letter, and perhaps the best extant on evangelization, noting that "harmony" is the work of the Holy Spirit, who is alone author of plurality and diversity. Fulfilling an early promise, on April 20 the postulator for the cause of Archbishop Romero, Archbishop Vicenzo Paglia, announced that Romero's cause for canonization had been unblocked so it could proceed. Brazilian liberation theologian Leonardo Boff said, "With this pope, a Jesuit and a pope from the Third World, we can breathe happiness....Pope Francis has both the vigor and tenderness that we need to create a new spiritual world."[22]

Pope Francis's first encyclical, *Lumen fidei*, appeared on July 5, 2013, but most of it was drafted by Pope Benedict. Pope Francis acknowledges in the introduction that Benedict had almost completed the first draft of the encyclical before his resignation, and that it was meant to supplement his earlier encyclicals on charity and hope. "I have taken up his fine work and added a few contributions of my own" (no. 7). The basic theme of the encyclical is that the light of faith provides a more comprehensive vision, a deeper understanding in a world where too often darkness reigns and secular reason is seen as sufficient. While this is a characteristic of Benedict's thought, and Francis would not disagree, many suspect they hear the voice of Francis in the following: "Faith is not a light which scatters all our darkness, but a lamp which guides our steps in the night and suffices for the journey....God does not provide arguments which explain everything; rather, his response is that of an accompanying presence, a history of goodness which touches every story of suffering and opens up a ray of light" (no. 57).

Much more representative of Francis's thought is his apostolic letter *Evangelii gaudium*, released on November 24, 2013. In it he calls for the conversion of the papacy, decentralization of the Vatican, and recognition of the authority or "juridical status" of episcopal conferences, which should include a genuine doctrinal authority (no. 32). Citing the concerns of episcopal conferences from Asia, Africa, and Latin America shows his collegial vision. He prefers a church "bruised, hurting and dirty" (no. 49), at the service of the poor, with a pastoral ministry transmitting not a multitude of doctrines (no. 35) but the saving love of God manifest in Jesus. And he pronounces a firm "no" to an economy of exclusion, inequality, and "trickle-down theories which assume that economic growth, encouraged by a free market, will inevitably succeed in bringing about greater justice and inclusiveness in the world. This opinion, which has never been confirmed by the facts, expresses a crude and naïve trust in the goodness of those wielding economic power and in the sacralized workings of the prevailing economic system" (no. 54).

OPENNESS TO CHANGE

Pope Francis seems open to change. He has said, "One does not remain faithful, like the traditionalists or the fundamentalists, to the letter. Fidelity is always openness to change, a blossoming, a growth, coming out of the garden of our own convictions." One of his favorite metaphors is that our certainties imprison not only ourselves, but also the Holy Spirit. He says that the Lord brings about change in those who are faithful to him. To illustrate, he refers to the story of Jonah, sent by God to preach to the Ninevites, who ran the other way because he didn't want to tell them, enemies of the Jews, of God's love for them. "He had fenced off his soul with the barbed wire of those certainties that instead of giving freedom with God and opening horizons of greater service to others had finished by deafening his heart....Our certainties can become a wall, a jail that imprisons the Holy Spirit."[23]

In his homily on April 16 at an early morning Mass in the chapel of his residence, Pope Francis said Christians must struggle with the temptation to tame the Holy Spirit. "We want the Holy Spirit to sleep," he said. "We want to domesticate the Holy Spirit, and that just won't do because he is God and he is that breeze that comes and goes, and you don't know from where." The Holy Spirit is God's strength, the pope said. The Holy Spirit "gives us consolation and the strength to move forward," and the moving forward part is what can be a bother. People think it's better to be comfortable, but that is not what the fire of the Holy Spirit brings. He said reactions to the Second Vatican Council are a prime example. "The council was a beautiful work of the Holy Spirit," he said. "But after 50 years, have we done everything the Holy Spirit in the council told us to do?...The answer, he said, is 'no.'"[24]

He speaks of the importance of consultation, even for the pope; he also suggests the need for change in the way church decisions are arrived at:

> The consistories [of cardinals], the synods [of bishops] are, for example, important places to make real

and active this consultation. We must, however, give them a less rigid form. I do not want token consultations, but real consultations. The consultation group of eight cardinals, this "outsider" advisory group, is not only my decision, but it is the result of the will of the cardinals, as it was expressed in the general congregations before the conclave. And I want to see that this is a real, not ceremonial consultation.[25]

We should not expect Pope Francis to be terribly liberal on those issues raised up in the so-called culture wars. As a Latin American, he will reflect the more conservative culture of the continent. But in his direct way of speaking and in his interviews and public addresses, he is changing the way the church addresses many of these questions.

He has been courageous in speaking out from his pulpit on behalf of the poor and the vulnerable in Argentina, saying that trampling on the dignity of a woman, a man, a child, the elderly, is a grave sin that cries out to heaven. In response, Argentine President Néstor Kirchner said, "Our God belongs to all, but watch out the devil also reaches everyone, those of us that wear pants and those that wear cassocks."[26] In the last ten years, the Argentine government has been "extremely liberal" on issues such as gay marriage and abortion, and Bergoglio has not been shy about criticizing its policies. Kirchner's successor, his wife, Cristina, has accused the cardinal of having a mind trapped in the Middle Ages. On the other hand, according to the *National Catholic Reporter*'s John Allen, Francis defends the idea of marriage as a union between a man and a woman but condemns "spiritual and pastoral harassment" of individuals and couples, suggesting that "a union of a private nature" among same-sex partners is another matter.[27]

Early in his pontificate, Archbishop Charles Chaput of

Philadelphia acknowledged that Catholics in the right wing of the church "generally have not been really happy" with some aspects of Francis's early months as pope. Some feel that he has been silent on abortion, gay marriage, and euthanasia.[28] Francis is aware that he has been criticized for not focusing on these issues. In an interview with the editor of *La Civiltà Cattolica*, he said: "We cannot insist only on issues related to abortion, gay marriage and the use of contraceptive methods. This is not possible. I have not spoken much about these things, and I was reprimanded for that. But when we speak about these issues, we have to talk about them in a context. The teaching of the church, for that matter, is clear and I am a son of the church, but it is not necessary to talk about these issues all the time."[29]

LITURGY

The new pope has already indicated his preferences for a more simple style, both liturgical and otherwise, standing rather than sitting on a throne to greet the cardinals after his election, simpler vestments, refusing to take the papal throne in Benedict's chapel when the two met the week after his election, suggesting instead that the two kneel side by side in the first pew because "we are brothers." While archbishop, he delivered a blistering attack on priests who refused to baptize children born out of wedlock, calling it "a rigorous and hypocritical neo-clericalism which also uses the sacraments as a tool to affirm its own supremacy."

Within days of his election, liturgical traditionalists were criticizing him for appearing on the balcony after his election in just the white cassock of the holy father, rather than in priestly vestments, and without the little white cape or *mozzetta*. Another said it was "the end of the reform of the reform." He celebrated the Holy Thursday liturgy in a prison for young people, washing and kissing the feet of the young inmates, two of them women. For years some bishops in the United States have refused to wash the feet of women in the Holy Thursday mandatum, arguing that the rubrics says "men" (*viri*), and because some see the Last Supper as a kind of ordination, which of course it is not; thus Francis shows his disregard for legalistic liturgical interpretations that seem to hinder the very purpose of the liturgy.

Just a week after his election, an article on a conservative website spoke of the new pope's "painful liturgies," contrasting his liturgical simplicity with what it called the "Benedictine reforms,"[30] and some have charged that he did not support the wider use of the Latin Tridentine liturgy in Argentina. He said in his 2013 interview, "I think the decision of Pope Benedict [his decision of July 7, 2007, to allow a wider use of the Tridentine Mass] was prudent and motivated by the desire to help people who have this sensitivity. What is worrying, though, is the risk of the ideologization of the *Vetus Ordo*, its exploitation."[31]

ECUMENISM

His election as Pope Francis was welcomed enthusiastically by evangelicals and Pentecostals in Argentina. The flagship evangelical magazine, *Christianity Today*, published a picture of Cardinal Bergoglio with papal preacher Father Raniero Cantalamessa, with the cardinal kneeling to receive a blessing from some twenty Protestant pastors at the Third Fraternal Encounter of the Renewed Communion of Evangelicals and Catholics in Buenos Aires, June 19, 2006. Virtually unprecedented, but traditionalists were upset. The next week, according to the book Bergoglio wrote with his friend Rabbi Abraham Skorka, *On Heaven and Earth*, a traditionalist magazine carried under the headline the subhead

"Buenos Aires *sede vacante*: Archbishop commits the sin of apostasy."

Another article featured an interview with international evangelist Luis Palau (a native of Argentina, now living in Portland, Oregon), who spoke of Bergoglio as a personal friend. Of the changes in Catholic/evangelical relations in Latin America with Pope Francis, he said that tensions will be eased: "There will be no confrontational style....He has proved it over and over in his term as the cardinal of Argentina. There was more building bridges and showing respect, knowing the differences, but majoring on what we can agree on: on the divinity of Jesus, his virgin birth, his resurrection, the second coming." The two like to drink maté together.[32]

The Anglican bishop of Argentina, Greg Venables, called Cardinal Jorge Bergoglio's election "an inspired choice." He said that after Pope Benedict XVI created a separate ordinariate for Anglicans, then-Cardinal Jorge Bergoglio reached out to him. Bergoglio made it clear that he values the place of Anglicans in the church universal. "He called me to have breakfast with him one morning and told me very clearly that the Ordinariate was quite unnecessary and that the church needs us as Anglicans."[33]

In mid-July of his first year in office, Pope Francis approved a modification to the ordinariate that allows some Catholics to join: "A person who has been baptized in the Catholic Church but who has not completed the sacraments of initiation, and subsequently returns to the faith and practice of the church as a result of the evangelizing mission of the ordinariate, may be admitted to membership and receive the sacrament of confirmation or the sacrament of the Eucharist or both." This means that the ordinariates are not just for former Anglicans, but participate in the wider mission of the Catholic Church and its New Evangelization.

Francis has also made significant gestures toward both the Jewish and Islamic communities. He was praised by Jewish leaders for his response after the 1994 bombing of the seven-story Jewish headquarters of Argentina's Jewish community, and in 2012 he opened his cathedral for a joint prayer service to commemorate the seventy-fourth anniversary of *Kristallnacht*, the night in 1938 in Hitler's Germany when so many synagogues were destroyed, Jewish stores looted, and Jews arrested or beaten. In November 2012 he hosted representatives of the Jewish, Muslim, evangelical, and Orthodox communities to pray for peace in the Middle East.

RELATIONS WITH THE JESUITS

Bergoglio was named Jesuit provincial of Argentina when he was just thirty-six years old, and the province at that time was very divided between more conservative Jesuits who wanted to reform the Society of Jesus, and others who were leaving traditional ministries, joining base communities, working directly with the poor, and becoming involved in various political movement's, some of them apparently with Marxist leanings. He tried to mediate between these extremes, and between the church and the government, though he was cautious about what could be seen as political involvement.

But in those days he himself was quite conservative, insisting on preconciliar songs at liturgy, clerical collars for students, and textbooks in Latin, and his style of governance was said to be authoritarian. Thus not all Jesuits were overjoyed to hear of his election. After becoming pope, he acknowledged that his "authoritarian and quick manner of making decisions led me to have serious problems and to be accused of being ultraconservative." But he added that he has never been a "right-winger," and that making him provincial when he was only thirty-six years old was "crazy."[34]

Some secular commentators have accused him of cooperating with the government during the 1976–83 "Dirty War," when some twenty-two thousand people, according to official records uncovered in 2006, and perhaps as high as thirty thousand, were "disappeared," often dropped out of helicopters over the ocean. They included politicians, teachers and professors, trade unionists, left-leaning writers, and Marxists guerillas opposed to the dictatorship. At the same time, perhaps as many as six thousand military personnel and supporters of the regime were killed by the guerillas. People lived in fear and many were victims of violence. Among the tragedies was the kidnapping of children of those accused of being leftists who were then given to other, more conservative or military families without children to raise.

Left-wing journalist Horacio Verbitsky accused Bergoglio of doing nothing to help two of his Jesuits, Fathers Orlando Yorio and Francisco Jalics, when he was provincial. The two priests were working in a *favela* or slum, and Bergoglio had warned them about some of their teachings. Arrested in 1976, the two were taken to the Navy Mechanics School where they were abused and tortured for five months before finally being released. Though the journalist argues that Bergoglio did nothing to help them, actually he was working behind the scenes to free them. He even arranged to say Mass in the junta leader's home by a stratagem, where he pleaded for their release.[35] They were freed and afterward both left the country.

Subsequently, one of the two left the Jesuits; the other, Father Jalics, later concelebrated a public Mass with Bergoglio after he was named archbishop of Buenos Aires and publicly embraced him. According to Vatican correspondent Andrea Tornielli, Verbitsky is a close friend of former Argentine

President Néstor Kirchner, whom Cardinal Bergoglio had criticized in 2005, so he may have a more personal agenda.[36] A
less biased account maintains that Bergoglio was transformed
by his experience during Argentina's "Dirty War."[37] Adolfo
Pérez Esquivel, who received the Nobel Peace Prize in 1980,
has said that Bergoglio had no links with the dictatorship and
was not complicit in their crimes.[38]

CONCLUSION

The Catholic Church has been blessed with two extraordinary popes in the opening decades of the twenty-first century. Pope Benedict XVI will be remembered for his
scholarship; seldom has the church had a pope so eminently
qualified as a theologian. He was also a public intellectual.
He has been named to the Académie Française, the Rhineland-
Westphalia Academy of Sciences, and the European Academy
of Sciences and Arts. His encyclicals, relatively brief and
readable, are rich in references to philosophers, social scientists, and novelists, not all of them Christians, as well as to
traditional works.

But his deepest interest has always been to bring others to
the love of God, who is both reason and love. As he says in his
encyclical *Deus caritas est*, "God is the absolute and ultimate
source of all being; but this universal principle of creation—
the *Logos*, primordial reason—is at the same time a lover with
all the passion of a true love" (no. 10). Being a Christian cannot be reduced to morality and it is more than theology; it
means entering into a relationship with the person of Jesus.
Thus he easily adopted his predecessor's language of a new
evangelization because it so well embraced his own concerns.
He has continued to insist that evangelization remains essential to the church's mission. In Benedict's emphasis on bring-

ing others into communion with the person of Christ, he will be remembered as a teacher for all the churches.

Pope Francis brings to his pontificate an evangelical simplicity and a direct, simple language, rooted in the gospel. But he also brings a theological sophistication to his ministry. In an address to the leadership of CELAM (the Latin American Episcopal Council), he outlined the temptations to a missionary discipleship so important for the church today. One is turning the gospel into some kind of ideology, whether through a sociological reductionism to Marxism or market liberalism, or psychologizing it by turning the encounter with Jesus into a immanent growth in self-awareness without a missionary spirit, or a Gnosticism that offers a disembodied, higher spirituality for the "enlightened" or the elite, or a Pelagian solution that seeks the restoration of outdated forms or "safe" theologies of a lost past. Other temptations include a functionalism that aims at efficiency, results, and statistics, as though the church were some kind of nongovernmental organization (NGO), or a clericalism that he sees as very present in Latin America, one that takes away freedom and maturity, diminishing lay responsibility.[39]

Time will tell how successful he will be in his mandate for the reform of the Roman Curia, but he has named eight cardinal advisers from around the world to assist him in this effort, and in his homilies and public statements, he speaks of a humble church, not focusing narrowly on doctrinal or sexual issues, but seeking out the lost. In an interview with Eugenio Scalfari, co-founder and former editor of the Italian newspaper *La Repubblica* and an avowed atheist, he criticized the Roman Curia for being too inward looking or "Vatican-centric." Though it "is not itself a court," he said, "courtiers can be found there."[40]

In one of his powerful images, Francis referred to the Book of Revelation, according to which Jesus says that he is

THIS IS OUR FAITH

at the door and knocks. "Obviously, the text refers to his knocking from the outside in order to enter, but I think about the times in which Jesus knocks from within so that we will let him come out. The self-referential church keeps Jesus Christ within herself and does not let him out."[41] Hopefully, Pope Francis can help change his church, to let Jesus out so that he might transform us and transform our world.

NOTES

1. See Jared Wicks, "Six Texts by Prof. Joseph Ratzinger as *Peritus* before and during Vatican Council II," *Gregorianum* 89/2 (2008).

2. Joseph Cardinal Ratzinger, *Introduction to Christianity* (London: Burns and Oates, 1969; originally published in German as *Einführung in das Christentum* in 1968).

3. Pope Benedict XVI, *Jesus of Nazareth*, vol. 1 (New York: Doubleday, 2007), 92.

4. Joseph Ratzinger, *Truth and Tolerance: Christian Belief and World Religions* (San Francisco: Ignatius Press, 2004), 252. See also Ratzinger, *Values in a Time of Upheaval* (San Francisco: Ignatius Press, 2006), 65–66.

5. Joseph Ratzinger, *Principles of Catholic Theology: Building Stones for a Fundamental Theology* (San Francisco: Ignatius Press, 1987), 53.

6. See Joseph Ratzinger, *Theological Highlights of Vatican II* (New York: Paulist Press, 2009; first published in German as four booklets after each session of the Council, 1962–65).

7. See Richard R. Gaillardetz, *The Church in the Making* (New York: Paulist Press, 2006), 128–29.

8. Thomas R. Rourke, *The Social and Political Thought of Benedict XVI* (New York: Rowman and Littlefield, 2011), 119.

9. Eric Vögelin, *The New Science of Politics* (Chicago: University of Chicago Press, 1995), 120. Vincent Twomey notes a direct influence of Vögelin's thought on Ratzinger; see his *Pope*

Benedict XVI: The Conscience of Our Age (San Francisco: Ignatius Press, 2007), 52n22.

10. *Dominus Iesus*, no. 18.

11. Ratzinger, *Principles of Catholic Theology*, 156.

12. John L. Allen, "2007's Neglected Story: Benedict XVI and Affirmative Orthodoxy" (Jan. 3, 2008); ncronline.org/node/11513.

13. James Corkery, *Joseph Ratzinger's Theological Ideas* (New York: Paulist Press, 2009), 109, see 109–24; also see Lieven Boeve, "Europe in Crisis: A Question of Belief or Unbelief? Perspectives from the Vatican," *Modern Theology* 23/2 (April 2007): 205–27.

14. John Thavis, "Vatican Intensifies Defence of Pope on Sex Abuse Decisions," *Catholic News Service* (March 29, 2010); see catholicnews.com/data/stories/cns/1001299.htm.

15. "Three Catholic Church Reformers Reflect on Latest Sexual Abuse Reports," http://www.nj.com/news/index.ssf/2010/03/three_catholic_church_reformer.html.

16. Pope Benedict XVI, "Meeting with the Bishops of the United States," April 16, 2008; see *Origins* 37/46 (2008): 737.

17. Cited in the Huffington Post at http://www.huffingtonpost.com/2013/02/11/pope-benedict-xvi-to-resi_n_2660670.html.

18. Stacy Meichtry and Alessandra Galloni, "Fifteen Days in Rome: How the Pope Was Picked," *Wall Street Journal* (April 12, 2013); see http://www.freerepublic.com/focus/religion/3007320/posts.

19. Jorge Mario Bergoglio and Abraham Skorka, *On Heaven and Earth: Pope Francis on Faith, Family, and the Church in the Twenty-First Century* (Colorado Springs, CO: Image Books/Random House, 2013), 50–51.

20. Quoted in Matthew B. Brunson, *Pope Francis* (Huntington, IN: Our Sunday Visitor, 2013), 154–55.

21. "What I Would Have Said at the Consistory," interview with Cardinal Jorge Mario Bergoglio by Stefania Falasca, *30Days* 11 (2007); see http://www.30giorni.it/articoli_id_16457_l3.htm.

22. Leonardo Boff, quoted in CathNewsUSA Newsletter (April 29, 2013).

23. See Andrea Tornielli, *Francis: Pope of a New World* (San Francisco: Ignatius Press, 2013), 117; see also 15.

24. Cindy Wooden, Catholic News Service, "Pope Says Catholics Still Need to Enact Teachings of Vatican II"; see http://www.catholicnews.com/data/stories/cns/1301701.htm.

25. Pope Francis, "A Big Heart Open to God: The Exclusive Interview with Pope Francis," *America* (September 30, 2013); http://americamagazine.org/pope-interview (brackets in original).

26. President Néstor Kirchner, quoted in Brunson, *Pope Francis*, 149.

27. John L. Allen Jr., "Book Indicates Pope is a Moderate Realist," *National Catholic Reporter* (April 19, 2013); see http://ncronline.org/blogs/all-things-catholic/book-indicates-pope-moderate-realist.

28. US News, "Chaput: Church's Right Wing 'Generally Not Happy' With the Pope," *CathNews USA* (July 25, 2013); see http://www.cathnewsusa.com/2013/07/chaput-churchs-right-wing-generally-not-happy-with-the-pope/.

29. Pope Francis, "A Big Heart Open to God."

30. Andrew M. Haines, "The Pope's Painful Liturgies," Catholic Online (March 21, 2013).

31. Pope Francis, "A Big Heart Open to God."

32. Melissa Steffan, "Luis Palau: Why It Matters that Pope Francis Drinks Mate with Evangelicals," interview at *Christianity Today* (March 14, 2013); see http://www.christianitytoday.com/ct/2013/march-web-only/luis-palau-pope-francis-drinks-mate-evangelicals-bergoglio.html?start=2.

33. Anglican Bishop of Argentina Greg Venables; see Meinrad Scherer-Emunds, "Will Pope Francis Revitalize Ecumenism and Interfaith Dialogue?" *U.S. Catholic*, http://www.uscatholic.org/blog/201303/will-pope-francis-revitalize-ecumenism-and-interfaith-dialogue-27051.

34. Pope Francis, "A Big Heart Open To God."

35. Brunson, *Pope Francis*, 133.

36. Tornielli, *Francis*, 102.

37. Paul Vallely, *Pope Francis: Untying the Knots* (London: Bloomsbury, 2013).

38. Adolfo Pérez Esquivel; see "'Bergoglio Had No Links with the Dictatorship,' Peace Nobel Prize Winner," *Buenos Aires Herald* (March 14, 2013), http://www.buenosairesherald.com/article/126367/.

39. Address to the Leadership of the Episcopal Conferences of Latin America during the General Coordination Meeting, July 28, 2013; http://w2.vatican.va/content/francesco/en/speeches/2013/july/documents/papa-francesco_20130728_gmg-celam-rio.html.

40. Francis X. Rocca, *Catholic News Service*, "Pope Calls for less 'Vatican-centric,' more socially conscious church" (October 1, 2013); http://www.catholicnews.com/data/stories/cns/1304129.htm.

41. Carol Glatz, "Church Must Not Be Self-Centred, Pope Francis Told Cardinals," *Catholic Herald.Co.uk* (March 28, 2013); see http://www.catholicherald.co.uk/news/2013/03/28/church-must-not-be-self-centred-pope-francis-told-cardinals/.

CHAPTER 9

GLOBAL CATHOLICISM

More than fifty years have passed since the Second Vatican Council opened in Rome. Where is the church today? Did the publication of the Council's sixteen constitutions, declarations, and decrees signify the completion of the renewal of the church that the Council represented, or did those documents mark only the beginning of a process that has not yet been completed? Did the Council mark a radical break with the past, precisely in its style of being church, as John O'Malley has argued, or was it in continuity with the past, as Cardinal Avery Dulles and Pope Benedict have insisted? These questions are still being debated.

In his famous *Ratzinger Report*, then–Cardinal Ratzinger wrote, "There is no 'pre-' or 'post-' conciliar Church: there is but one, unique Church that walks the path toward the Lord."[1] But if the Catholic Church remains the same, in basic continuity with its long tradition, its faith, and its doctrine, John O'Malley sees the Council as having initiated a new way of presenting itself to the world. At the Second Vatican Council, the church abandoned the "terse, technical, juridical, and punitive language of other councils" and began speaking in a style that was invitational, stressing dialogue, collegiality, and partnership.[2] In the Pastoral Constitution on the Church in the Modern World (*Gaudium et spes*), the church saw itself at the service of the world.

THE BATTLE FOR MEANING

A recent book by Massimo Faggioli argues that there has been an ongoing "clash of narratives" over the meaning of the Council. Rather than a battle between conservatives and liberals, as it has often been described, Faggioli, among others, sees it as a conflict between neo-Augustinians, whose perspective is more Platonic, and neo-Thomists, who are philosophically closer to Aristotle. The neo-Augustinians (among them Joseph Ratzinger, Henri de Lubac, Jean Daniélou, Hans Urs von Balthasar, and Louis Boyer) tend to see the world in a negative light, abounding in sin and evil. Rather than being open to the world, the church should be more suspicious and distrustful toward it.

On the other hand, the neo-Thomists or post–Vatican II Thomists (Yves Congar, Marie-Dominique Chenu, Edward Schillebeeckx, and to a lesser extent, Karl Rahner and Bernard Lonergan) are more progressive and more open to the world. They were agreed on the importance of history as crucial for theological work and saw modern philosophy and social sciences as playing the role that Aristotle's work had played for Thomas in the thirteenth century. Still, some, like Rahner, remained more cautious.[3]

There have been two significant milestones in the battle over the meaning of the Council since 1985. The first was the 1985 Extraordinary Synod of Bishops, called by Pope John Paul II. Indeed, it was a turning point, as from this point on the neo-Augustinian appraisal of Vatican II began its ascendency. John Paul's interpretation of Vatican II was more progressive *ad extra*, in social teaching, ecumenism, and interreligious dialogue, but at the same time was more conservative *ad intra*, that is, in regard to the church's inner life.

The second milestone was a talk Pope Benedict XVI gave to the Roman Curia on December 5, 2005, shortly after his election to the chair of Peter. In it he contrasted a "hermeneutic of discontinuity and rupture" with a "hermeneutic of reform,"[4] arguing against appeals to the "spirit" of the Council instead of seeing its work embodied, and thus complete, in the Council's texts. Since 1985 the notion of the church as the "people of God" lost ground, the idea of a "universal catechism" was revived, the notion of "collegiality" was more or less limited to the relationship between the pope and the bishops, rather than to the "partial realizations" of collegiality such as the synod of bishops, episcopal conferences, and the *ad limina* visits, while the Roman Curia was now seen as responsible for the "institutional reception" of the Council.[5] Other areas that have been reinterpreted or developed in a more conservative direction include the way "subsists in" in *Lumen gentium*, no. 8, has been interpreted, to identify the church of Christ with the Catholic Church, and the "reform of the reform" of the liturgy, evident in the new English translation of the Roman Missal.

On a more popular level, Catholics have been divided about what the Council meant for the church. Some Catholics feel that the church has gone too far too fast, accommodating itself to the spirit of the times rather than challenging the times with its timeless truth. The late Archbishop Marcel Lefebvre's Society of St. Pius X is the most prominent of the rejectionist groups. Other Catholics today are equally unhappy, but for the opposite reasons. They feel that the church has not moved fast enough, that it has failed to carry out the reforms that were indicated by the Council documents, that a reaction has set in which seeks to restore the closed and centralized Catholicism of an earlier era.

But for the vast majority of Catholics throughout the world, Vatican II belongs now to history, and the changes it introduced into Catholic life are taken for granted. In more technical language, the Council has been "received" by the church. However one answers the question about the meaning of Vatican II, one thing is certain: the currents of renewal that preceded the Council, as well as new ones that the Council unleashed, continue their reshaping of contemporary Catholicism.

In a real sense, the issues raised by these currents constitute the Council's unfinished agenda. And they have a great deal to do with a number of challenges that, depending on how they are resolved, could radically affect the church's future. These challenges include the shortage of priests; the related issues of clerical celibacy and the right of communities to the Eucharist (a phrase Pope Benedict rejected, because it suggested, in his view, the notion that the community can confer the Eucharist on itself, without an ordained presider);[6] a more collegial style of church leadership, allowing the laity some participation in its decision-making processes, particularly important in the recent sexual abuse crisis and in the formulation of doctrine; addressing the special concerns of women, minorities, the divorced, and those in mixed marriages; renewing its ethical teaching, particularly in the area of sexuality; taking some practical steps toward the reconciliation of churches; allowing for greater adaptation and inculturation at local levels and in different cultures; and becoming a more evangelical church.

CHALLENGES FOR A WORLD CHURCH

Karl Rahner described Vatican II as the church's first self-actualization as a world church, for it represented the first gathering of a genuinely indigenous episcopate, unlike Vatican I (1869–70), where most of the bishops from Asia or Africa were European or North American missionary bishops. Vatican II brought together bishops from 116 different countries, most of them native born, though 48 percent were from Europe or North America.[7] But by the 1985 Extraordinary Synod of Bishops in Rome, 74 percent of the bishops came from countries other than those in Europe or North America, as do more than 70 percent of the world's Catholics today. At the 2005 Synod on the Eucharist, the 244 bishops participating came from 118 countries.

A New Center of Gravity

These demographic changes mean that Catholicism's center of gravity has shifted from Europe and North America to the global South, bringing new challenges to the church, and new tensions. While the global population increased by 117 percent in this period, Catholics increased by 139 percent, growing by 278 percent in Asia alone. Similarly, while some 2,500 bishops attended Vatican II, today's episcopate numbers 4,451, with 14 percent from Africa, 40 percent from the Americas, 13 percent from Asia, 30 percent from Europe, and 3 percent from Oceania.

It is estimated that by 2050, 75 percent of the world's Catholics will live south of the equator. As these postcolonial churches of Asia, Latin America, and Africa begin to find their own voices, developing their own "contextual" theologies to address local problems, there may well be more tensions between them and Rome, some of which have long been evident.

Postcolonial Churches

In Latin America, liberation theology is no longer an issue, as Roman appointments of more conservative bishops under Pope John Paul II changed the once energized Conference of Latin American Bishops (CELAM), with its option for the poor. But the poor have a new advocate in Pope Francis, and on September 11, 2013, the pope met informally in the Domus Sanctae Marthae with Dominican Father Gustavo Gutiérrez, universally recognized as the father of liberation theology.

Another important phenomenon is what some call the "Pentecostalization" of the Latin American Catholic Church, particularly through the widespread Catholic Charismatic Renewal. By the early twenty-first century, the renewal had grown to nearly 120 million participants, with more than 60 percent of them in Latin America. While these Catholics "report holding beliefs and having religious experiences that are typical of Pentecostal or spirit-filled movements," they appear able to incorporate renewalist or charismatic practices without displacing their Catholic identity and core beliefs and most do so without formal participation in Catholic charismatic organizations.[8]

While the Catholic Charismatic Renewal is a popular movement, especially among the poor, it has also touched members of the hierarchy. The fifth Conference of Latin American Bishops (CELAM) at Aparecida (2007) launched a "continental mission" that adopted, to a considerable extent, evangelical/Pentecostal language in its documents. "Words such as 'mission' (140 times), 'Spirit' (149), 'encounter with Jesus' (47), 'conversion' (46), 'experience' (44), 'joy' (73), and 'fire' (7) strike the reader as uncommon within a Catholic context, and as a possible sign of the influence of Pentecostal and Charismatic theology."[9] Many see the election of Pope Francis, the first pope from Latin America and the global South, as a sign of hope.

African churches, still trying to shake off the remains of colonialism, are concerned with integrating practices from popular religion, though the Catholic Church in Africa has tended to be quite conservative, often "more Roman than the pope." But a new generation of theologians, with women prominent among them, is emerging in Africa who will speak for a truly African Church. "African women are leading the way not only in formulating a critical appraisal of the ecclesiastical status quo, but also in articulating alternatives to an inherited theology and discourse that favors patriarchy and clericalism."[10]

Asian churches in particular have struggled to address their own concerns. At the 1998 Synod of Bishops for Asia, the Asian Episcopal Conferences criticized the Roman-drafted outline document as being too Western in its approach. The Japanese bishops wondered why they should have to obtain Roman approval for Japanese translations of liturgical and catechetical texts. Indian bishops argued for the right of local churches to develop their own methods and expressions for preaching the gospel. The Indonesian Episcopal Conference has several times asked Rome for permission to ordain married men to meet its acute shortage of priests, without success. Some members were resentful of instructions from curial officials to avoid the word *subsidiarity* on the debatable grounds that it was not a theological term. Many of the bishops, concerned about interreligious dialogue, objected that the curial emphasis on the uniqueness of Christ was not a good starting point in an Asian context because it left non-Christians feeling humiliated.[11] They pointed out that the Roman document ignored the experience of their conferences in regard to evangelization. Their concern was *how* Christ was proclaimed, and they spoke of a "triple dialogue," with other religions, with culture, and with the poor. In the Philippines, the late Jesuit bishop Francisco Claver wrote that the efforts of the bishops of the Philippines to embrace the communion ecclesiology of

Vatican II encountered great resistance during the pontificate of Pope John Paul II.[12]

What is happening religiously in China is not always easy to track, but Christianity is growing exponentially. According to various estimates, the public (official) Catholic Church, under the supervision of the Chinese Patriotic Association, has about 5.3 million members and the underground church between 12 and 14 million members. At the opening of the twenty-first century, there were twenty-four major seminaries operating with government permission and another ten in the underground church. There are over forty novitiates for sisters in the open church and twenty in the underground church.

Protestant Christians are estimated at 39 million, though some estimates vary between 20 and 130 million if the rapidly growing "house churches" are considered.[13] It has been estimated that the overwhelming majority of Christians are at least charismatic but also Pentecostal in their theological orientation; this includes 90 percent of house-church Christians and perhaps 80 percent of the total Christian population. Classical Pentecostals represent a minority but are still 25 percent of house-church Christians.[14] Unfortunately, I am not aware of any efforts to build bridges between these house-church Christians and China's Roman Catholics, a situation made worse by the fact that the government considers Catholics and Protestants as separate religions.

DIFFERENT CONCERNS

As the church's center of gravity shifts to the global South, those Catholics have very different concerns. As John Allen points out in *The Future Church*, the church of the global South will be largely non-Western, non-white, and non-affluent, and many would add, Pentecostal. It will be more evangelical; morally conservative, especially on sexual issues; liberal on social justice; suspicious of free-market capitalism and the global dominance of the West; antiwar and pro United Nations; more biblical and evangelical in engaging cultural issues; more concerned with a strong Catholic identity in the face of religious pluralism than with secularism; more concerned with indigenous religious practices; younger and more optimistic.[15]

EUROPE AND AMERICA

In the eyes of many of those in the global South, the concerns of the Church in the West, meaning Europe and North America, are more intramural: a married priesthood, the ordination of women, birth control, homosexuality and same-sex marriage, the reform of the structures of authority, the liturgy, the right to dissent, doctrinal reform. Many of these focus on the exercise of authority. Under Pope John Paul II, authority and decision making were recentered in Rome, increasing the power of the Roman Curia, and this dynamic had not changed under Pope Benedict XVI. Rather than being at the service of the pope and the bishops in the government of the church, the curia occupies a position between the bishops and the pope, diminishing the ability of the bishops to act as they judge best for their churches. Canonist Les Orsy observes that the structures and norms imposed on the episcopacy reveal "a deep theological imbalance in the life of the church: the function of the episcopate has been taken over to a great extent by the primacy."[16]

The church in the United States has experienced a significant loss of members. According to a Pew Forum Study (June 2008), more than one-quarter (28 percent) of Americans have left the faith in which they were raised for another religious tradition. Among these traditions, Catholicism has experienced the greatest net losses in members. While nearly one in three Americans (31 percent) were raised in the Catholic faith, today fewer than one in four (24 percent) continue to identify themselves as Catholic. Approximately one-third of the survey respondents who say they were raised Catholic no longer describe themselves as Catholic.[17] This means that roughly 10 percent of all Americans are former Catholics, a percentage much higher among people in their twenties and early thirties, according to John Cusick.[18] Former Catholics constitute the second largest "Christian group" in the United States, ahead of the Southern Baptists.

At the same time, these statistics can be deceptive, as Mark Gray and Joseph Harris have pointed out. The Catholic Church is the largest in terms of net losses, but it is also the largest Christian community in the United States. The numbers would be even worse if the Catholic Church were losing members at the rate of the other Christian churches. For example, 68 percent of those raised Catholic have remained in the faith, in comparison to 40 percent of Presbyterians, 45 percent of Episcopalians, and 47 percent of Pentecostals.[19]

There are similar losses being registered in other countries. In Austria approximately 600,000 Catholics have left the church since Cardinal Hans Herman Groer was accused of abusing a minor in 1995, culminating in the Austrian Church Referendum, a national dialogue of bishops and delegates that took place at Salzburg for three days in 1998. Recently, four hundred Austrian priests have raised the same issues, signing a "Declaration of Disobedience" saying that they would give communion to Catholics who are divorced and remarried and to Christians from other churches, allow competent lay Catholics to preach, and use every opportunity to speak in favor of the ordination of women and married men. What this amounts to is an open rebellion by one-tenth of the country's priests.[20]

In Germany in 2010 there were 170,339 Catholic baptisms and 181,193 departures from the church. In his September 2011 visit to Germany, Pope Benedict said that the problem was not structures but not enough faith. The once-proud Irish church, which dominated Irish society for years, is also in trouble. Divorce only became legal in Ireland in 1995. But the church has been dealt a terrible blow by the sexual-abuse scandal, and by government-sponsored reports detailing how bishops covered up cases of abuse to protect the church from scandal and the offending priests from the courts. After the release of the Cloyne Report in 2011, the prime minister publicly rebuked the Vatican from Parliament, and the Holy See withdrew its ambassador. In such a once Catholic society, the practice of the faith has dropped dramatically. Dublin Archbishop Dairmuid Martin estimates that only 18 percent of Catholics in his diocese attend Mass every week. Even the church in Poland is experiencing difficulties; the church has been slow to deal realistically with emerging reports of sexual abuse by clergy, refusing to remove offending priests from ministry.

RELIGIOUS PLURALISM

An era of globalization has seen religious fundamentalism and the violence that often flows from it as a growing problem. This means that interreligious dialogue has become increasingly important. Since Vatican II, Catholic theology has been concerned to rearticulate Christian faith in the context of religious pluralism. This was due at least in part to the Council itself. Vatican II moved Catholicism beyond the old axiom "no salvation outside the church" to teach the universal availability of God's grace (LG 16), and it brought Catholics to a new respect for the great world religions, teaching that the church rejects nothing that is true and holy in them; indeed, they often reflect a ray of truth that enlightens all peoples (NA 2).

The Council's steps in this direction have been significant, strengthening Catholicism for dialogue. Catholic scholars can enter into dialogue with a genuine respect for the religious "other," which makes dialogue a genuinely religious undertaking, open to the divine truth that may be reflected there. Without it, one attempts to dialogue with the presupposition that those who follow different religious traditions walk in darkness and error and cannot be saved without a conscious acceptance of Christ.

Religious pluralism is a crucial issue for the churches of Asia, living as they do as minority churches. The Federation of Asian Bishops Conferences (FABC) has developed an understanding of the church's mission in Asia as one of dialogue in the context of religious pluralism and placed witnessing to the kingdom of God at the heart of its mission. In the FABC documents, religious diversity is seen, not as something regrettable, but as a positive value that represents a richness and strength, for God's spirit is at work in all religious traditions, and all represent visions of the divine mystery. The proclamation of Jesus Christ in an Asian context means first of all witnessing to the values of the kingdom; this is the first call of the churches in Asia.[21] The 1990 Fifth Plenary Assembly of FABC pointed out that the challenge in Asia is "to proclaim the Good News of the Kingdom of God: to promote the values of the Kingdom such as justice, peace, love, compassion, equality and brotherhood in these Asian realities. In short, it is to make the Kingdom of God a reality."[22]

More problematically, the new context of religious pluralism has led in some places to a revised Christology in which Jesus appears more as exemplar than as universal savior, as well as a new ecclesiology and understanding of the

193

THIS IS OUR FAITH

church's mission as one of witnessing to the kingdom, along with the other world religions, with the effect of separating the kingdom from Christ and his salvific work. This has resulted in a revision of traditional Christology, a decentering of the church, and a new "regnocentric" emphasis on the kingdom of God.

For Edward Schillebeeckx and Roger Haight, Jesus is no longer the efficient cause of salvation, but rather its revealer or exemplary cause.[23] From the perspective of soteriology or the doctrine of salvation, the story of Jesus is increasingly seen, not as something Jesus accomplished, bringing about reconciliation and communion between God and humankind as in traditional soteriology, making him constitutive of our salvation, but as an example or model, showing us the way to God by his obedience to the Father and life of generous service. Paul Lakeland is sympathetic to those who see Jesus more as the way to God rather than as redeeming us through some kind of metaphysical act.

Though Peter Phan's missiological vision is always explicitly trinitarian, he argues that the mission of the church should not be seen as "ecclesiocentric," working to implant the church where it has not yet taken root, but as "regnocentric," witnessing to the kingdom of God, spreading gospel values—God's presence in Jesus bringing forgiveness and reconciliation, justice and peace throughout the world. In such a kingdom-centered ecclesiology, "no longer is the church considered the pinnacle or the very center of the Christian life. Rather it is moved from the center to the periphery and from the top to the bottom."[24] Like John the Baptist before Jesus, the church should say "the reign of God must increase, and I must decrease."[25]

Vatican reaction to these theologies of religious pluralism has not been slow in coming. The Congregation for the Doctrine of the Faith (CDF) has investigated the works of

Haight, Phan, Sobrino, and Jacques Dupuis. Its 2000 declaration *Dominus Iesus* was drafted largely in response to Asian theology and its approach to evangelization. The declaration insists both on "the unicity and salvific universality of the mystery of Jesus Christ" (no. 13) and on the inseparability of the kingdom of God from Christ or from the church (no. 18). Cardinal Joseph Ratzinger, under whose CDF presidency *Dominus Iesus* was issued, objects to any effort to make salvation something *within* history, rather than *beyond* it, or of reducing the church to a church of the poor, with a mission primarily social rather than one based on hierarchical mediation.[26] Thus, he specifically rejects "regnocentism" as an interpretation of the kingdom as a world of peace, justice, and respect for creation that can unite the different religions in a joint effort toward a common task. From this perspective, salvation becomes the work of human beings, a utopian messianism, not the work of God.[27]

CONCLUSION

The Catholic Church, now in the third millennium, is very different from what it was as the last century began. As we look back on those years since the Council, not all the news is good. In Europe and North America, many are discouraged, even disaffected. They sense an effort to reverse the Council's reforms, or at least to blunt them. The new English translation of the liturgy, much of it done secretly, is a case in point. Many also feel excluded, among them women, those with same-sex attractions, and youth. Internationally, we have seen tensions between local churches and Rome, as authority and decision making have become more centralized and top down. Number one on the cardinals' agenda at the conclave that elected Cardinal

Bergoglio as Pope Francis was the reform of the Roman Curia, and he has appointed eight cardinals from around the world to assist him in this task.

But there is also much good news. As the world's oldest institution, indeed the first truly global institution, changing the course of the Catholic Church is neither easy nor quickly done. It is already a world church, with a developed social teaching, international structures, religious orders and lay movements, synods of the worldwide episcopate, and a universal spokesman in the person of the pope. It continues to grow in the global South and in the United States, and elsewhere the church has vital congregations and an engaged laity.

Second, the Catholic Church is uniquely positioned to witness to the kingdom of God in an era characterized by globalization. In such a world, the Catholic Church is quintessentially a transnational actor (John Coleman), a primary agent and subject of globalization for at least as long as any other body (David Ryall), at the vanguard to the global human rights revolution (Samuel Huntington).[28] But without its faithful, what Pope John Paul liked to refer to as the "Christifideles," it cannot accomplish anything.

Third, the ministerial culture of the church has changed dramatically, with an energizing of the laity, at least in the United States. The explosion of lay ministries was unanticipated by the Council. The U.S. church as of 2010 has some 38,000 lay ecclesial ministers paid for at least twenty hours per week. Of these, 80 percent are women. There are another 18,493 in formation, with 62 percent women. The total number of priests is 39,993, with the average age about 65, and there are only 3,483 in seminaries and theologate programs. There will soon be more professional lay ministers in our parishes than priests, if it is not already true. Nearly half of all individuals on parish staffs are laywomen;

only 18 percent are priests.[29] This clearly says something about the future of ministry, and about women in ministry.

Fourth, institutionally, the church has a rich legacy of teaching on social justice, often referred to as "our best kept secret."[30] But Catholic leaders in the United States need to draw on the fullness of the Catholic tradition. A narrow focus on so-called family values, reducing the church's social concern to anti-abortion and same-sex marriages, impoverishes that tradition. Catholics need to be as committed to economic justice—including the ever-widening gap between the affluent and the poor; healthcare for the poor and disadvantaged; the rights of immigrants, refugees, and the victims of human trafficking and modern-day slavery (reportedly the most profitable global industry after the illegal arms trade); and ending the death penalty—as they are to the right to life of the unborn.

A final caution: Americans especially have to be careful not to identify their concerns with those of global Catholicism. As John Allen points out, American Catholics constitute only 6 percent of the global Catholic population.[31] For many Catholics in the global South, always in a minority status, Catholic identity is more important than church reform or adapting Catholic identity and doctrine in conversation with other religious traditions. As disciples, not just reformers or social engineers, we need to keep our eyes fixed on Jesus. The church is more than an experience of community or a place of worship. Its mission cannot be reduced to promoting the social gospel. In Latin America, where thousands have left the Catholic Church, it is frequently said that the church chose the poor, while the poor chose the Pentecostals.

While there is much to do in the area of social justice, evangelization remains essential to the church's mission. The church has a message, a gospel that needs to be heard. It makes the transcendent immanent, bringing the numinous into the midst of the human, disclosing it in symbol and rite, joining time and eternity. The risen Jesus is not just remembered but encountered in a holy communion, an intimate sharing in his body and blood, safeguarded by a tradition that claims continuity with the earliest Christian communities and ultimately with Jesus, God's Word become flesh. This is at the heart of the message the Catholic Church brings to the world.

NOTES

1. Joseph Ratzinger with Vittorio Messori, *The Ratzinger Report* (San Francisco: Ignatius Press, 1985), 35.

2. John W. O'Malley, *What Happened at Vatican II?* (Cambridge, MA: Harvard University Press, 2008), 11.

3. See Massimo Faggioli, *Vatican II: The Battle for Meaning* (Collegeville, MN: Liturgical Press, 2010), 66–83.

4. "Address of His Holiness Benedict XVI to the Roman Curia," December 22, 2005; see "Interpreting Vatican II," *Origins* 35/32 (January 26, 2006): 536.

5. Faggioli, *Vatican II*, 87.

6. Joseph Ratzinger, *Principles of Catholic Theology* (San Francisco: Ignatius Press, 1987), 287.

7. O'Malley, *What Happened at Vatican II?*, 23; see also Faggioli, *Vatican II*, 183.

8. Pew Forum Survey, "Changing Faiths: Latinos and the Transformation of American Religion" (April 25, 2007); http://www.pewforum.org/2007/04/25/changing-faiths-latinos-and-the-transformation-of-american-religion-2/.

9. Jacob Egeris Thorsen, "Charismatic Practice and Catholic Parish Life: A Qualitative and Theological Study of the Incipient Pentecostalization of the Church in Guatemala," PhD dissertation (Aarhus University, Denmark, 2012), 192.

10. Agbonkhianmeghe E. Orobator, "Out of Africa," *America* 207/13 (November 5, 2012): 19.

11. See Peter C. Phan, *The Asian Synod: Texts and Commentaries* (Maryknoll, NY: Orbis Books, 2002).

12. Francisco F. Claver, *The Making of a Local Church* (Maryknoll, NY: Orbis Books, 2008), 25–26.

13. Benoît Vermander, SJ, "Religious Revival and Exit from Religion in Contemporary China," *China Perspectives* [Online], 2009/4; http://chinaperspectives.revues.org/4917.

14. Luke Wesley, "Is the Chinese Church Predominantly Pentecostal," *Asian Journal of Pentecostal Studies* 7/2 (2004): 225–54.

15. John L. Allen, *The Future Church: How Ten Trends Are Revolutionizing the Catholic Church* (New York: Doubleday, 2009), 432–35.

16. Ladislas Orsy, *Receiving the Council* (Collegeville, MN: Liturgical Press, 2009), 30.

17. Pew Research, Religion and Public Life Project, "Religious Landscape Survey" (2007); http://pewresearch.org/pubs/743/united-states-religion.

18. "Priest Calls for New Strategies to Keep Young Adults in Church," *Catholic News Service* (May 6, 2008); http://www.catholicnews.com/data/stories/cns/0802495.htm.

19. Center for Applied Research in the Apostolate (CARA), "The Impact of Religious Switching and Secularization of the U.S. Adult Catholic Population" (2008); http://cara.georgetown.edu/caraservices/frstats/winter2008.pdf.

20. Christa Pongratz-Lippitt, "Revolt in the Ranks," *The Tablet*, September 10, 2011; http://archive.thetablet.co.uk/article/10th-september-2011/4/revolt-in-the-ranks.

21. Jonathan Y. Tan, "*Missio inter Gentes*: Towards a New Paradigm in the Mission Theology of the Federation of Asian Bishops' Conferences" (FABC), 71–74; http://www.jonathantan.org/essays/Missio%20Inter%20Gentes.pdf.

22. Cited by Tan, "*Missio inter Gentes*," 81; see *FABC V*, art. 1.7, in Gaudencio B. Rosales and Catalino G. Arévalo, eds. *For All the Peoples of Asia: Federation of Asian Bishops' Conferences Documents From 1970–1991* (Maryknoll, NY: Orbis Books, 1992), 275.

23. Edward Schillebeeckx, "The Religious and the Human Ecumene," in *The Future of Liberation Theology: Essays in Honor*

of Gustavo Gutiérrez, ed. Marc H. Ellis and Otto Maduro (Maryknoll, NY: Orbis Books, 1989), 183–85; Roger Haight, *The Future of Christology* (New York: Continuum, 2007), 70.

24. Peter C. Phan, "A New Way of Being Church: Perspectives from Asia," in *Governance, Accountability, and the Future of the Catholic Church*, ed. Francis Oakley and Bruce Russett (New York: Continuum, 2004), 183.

25. Peter C. Phan, *In Our Own Tongues: Perspectives from Asia on Mission and Inculturation* (Maryknoll, NY: Orbis Books, 2003), 37.

26. See Thomas P. Rausch, *Pope Benedict XVI: An Introduction to His Theological Vision* (New York: Paulist Press, 2009), 53–54.

27. Joseph Ratzinger/Pope Benedict XVI, *Jesus of Nazareth* (New York: Doubleday, 2007), 53–54.

28. John A. Coleman, ed., *Globalization and Catholic Social Thought* (Maryknoll, NY: Orbis Books, 2005), 20–22.

29. CARA, "The Changing Face of U.S. Catholic Parishes," *Origins* 41/12 (2011): 195; see also Center for Applied Research in the Apostolate, "Frequently Requested Church Statistics," http://cara.georgetown.edu/CARAServices/requestedchurchstats.html.

30. Michael J. Schultheis, Edward P. DeBerri, and Peter J. Henriot, *Our Best Kept Secret: The Rich Heritage of Catholic Social Teaching* (Washington, DC: Center of Concern, 1987).

31. John L. Allen, *The Future Church: How Ten Trends Are Revolutionizing the Catholic Church* (New York: Doubleday, 2009), 11.

BIBLIOGRAPHY

BASIC REFERENCE WORKS

Achtemeier, Paul J., ed. *HarperCollins Bible Dictionary*. San Francisco: HarperSanFrancisco, 1996.

Brown, Raymond E., Joseph Fitzmyer, and Roland Murphy, eds. *The New Jerome Biblical Commentary*. Englewood Cliffs, NJ: Prentice Hall, 1990.

Catechism of the Catholic Church. 2nd ed. Washington, DC: United States Catholic Conference, 1994.

Downey, Michael, ed. *The New Dictionary of Catholic Spirituality*. Collegeville, MN: Liturgical Press, 1993.

Komonchak, Joseph A., Mary Collins, and Dermot Lane, eds. *The New Dictionary of Theology*. Wilmington, DE: Michael Glazier, 1987.

McBrien, Richard P. *Catholicism*. San Francisco: Harper-SanFrancisco, 1994.

———, ed. *The HarperCollins Encyclopedia of Catholicism*. San Francisco: HarperSanFrancisco, 1995.

McKenzie, John L. *Dictionary of the Bible*. New York: Macmillan, 1965.

OTHER WORKS

Allen, John L., Jr. *The Future Church: How Ten Trends Are Revolutionizing the Catholic Church.* New York: Doubleday, 2009.

Brown, Raymond E. *An Introduction to the New Testament.* New York: Doubleday, 1997.

Brown, Raymond E. and John P. Meier. *Antioch and Rome: New Testament Cradles of Catholic Christianity.* New York: Paulist Press, 1983.

Connelly, John. *From Enemy to Brother: The Revolution in Catholic Teaching on the Jews 1933–1965.* Cambridge, MA: Harvard University Press, 2012.

Daly, Gabriel. *Transcendence and Immanence: A Study of Catholic Modernism and Integralism.* Oxford: Clarendon Press, 1980.

Doyle, Dennis M., *Communion Ecclesiology: Vision and Versions.* Maryknoll, NY: Orbis Books, 2000.

Dulles, Avery. *Models of the Church.* New York: Doubleday, 1974.

Dunn, James D. G. *Jesus and the Spirit.* Philadelphia: Westminster Press, 1975.

Faggioli, Massimo. *Vatican II: The Battle for Meaning.* Collegeville, MN: Liturgical Press, 2010.

Flynn, Gabriel, and Paul D. Murray, eds. *Ressourcement: A Movement for Renewal in Twentieth-Century Catholic Theology.* Oxford: Oxford University Press, 2012.

Gaillardetz, Richard R. *Ecclesiology for a Global Church.* Maryknoll, NY: Orbis Books, 2008.

Gaillardetz, Richard R., and Catherine Clifford. *Keys to the Council: Unlocking the Teaching of Vatican II.* Collegeville, MN: Liturgical Press, 2012.

Greeley, Andrew. *The Catholic Imagination.* Berkeley: University of California Press, 2000.

Harrington, Daniel J. *Jesus: A Historical Portrait.* Cincinnati, OH: St. Anthony Messenger Press, 2007.

Hastings, Adrian, ed. *Modern Catholicism: Vatican II and After.* New York: Oxford University Press, 1991.

Haught, John F. *God and the New Atheism: A Critical Response to Dawkins, Harris, and Hitchens.* Louisville, KY: Westminster John Knox Press, 2008.

Hertling, Ludwig. *Communio: Church and Papacy in Early Christianity.* Chicago: Loyola University Press, 1972.

Hurtado, Larry W. *Lord Jesus Christ: Devotion of Jesus in Earliest Christianity.* Grand Rapids, MI: William B. Eerdmans, 2003.

Johnson, Luke Timothy. *The Creed: What Christians Believe and Why It Matters.* New York: Doubleday, 2003.

Kasper, Walter. *That They May All Be One: The Call to Unity Today.* London: Burns & Oates, 2004.

LaCugna, Catherine Mowry. *God for Us: The Trinity and Christian Life.* San Francisco: HarperSanFrancisco, 1999.

Lohfink, Gerhard. *Jesus of Nazareth; What He Wanted, Who He Was.* Collegeville, MN: Liturgical Press, 2012.

McCarthy, Timothy G. *The Catholic Tradition: The Church in the Twentieth Century.* Chicago: Loyola Press, 1998.

McDermot, Brian. *Word Become Flesh: Dimensions of Christology.* Collegeville, MN: Liturgical Press, 1993.

O'Malley, John W. *What Happened at Vatican II.* Cambridge, MA: Harvard University Press, 2008.

O'Meara, Thomas F. *Theology of Ministry.* New York: Paulist Press, 1999.

Power, David N. *The Eucharistic Mystery: Revitalizing the Tradition.* New York: Crossroad, 1992.

Ratzinger, Joseph. *The Feast of Faith.* San Francisco: Ignatius Press, 1986.

Ratzinger, Joseph/Pope Benedict XVI. *Jesus of Nazareth*, 3 vols. New York: Doubleday, 2007; San Francisco: Ignatius, 2011; New York: Doubleday, 2012.

Rausch, Thomas P. *Catholicism in the Third Millennium*. Collegeville, MN: Liturgical Press, 2003.

————. *Pope Benedict XVI: An Introduction to his Theological Vision*. New York: Paulist Press, 2009.

Sullivan, Francis A. *The Church We Believe In: One, Holy, Catholic, and Apostolic*. New York: Paulist Press, 1988.

————. *Salvation outside the Church? Tracing the History of the Catholic Response*. New York: Paulist Press, 1992.

Spadaro, Antonio. "A Big Heart Open to God: A Conversation with Pope Francis," *America* 209/8 (September 30, 2013).

Tilley, Terrence. *The Disciples Jesus: Christology as Reconciling Practice*. Maryknoll, NY: Orbis Books, 2008.

Vallely, Paul. *Pope Francis: Untying the Knots*. London: Bloomsbury, 2013.

TO REORDER YOUR UPS DIRECT THERMAL LABELS:

1. Access our supply ordering website at **UPS.COM**®
   or contact UPS at 800-877-8652

2. Please refer to Label # 01774006 when ordering.

Shipper agrees to the UPS Terms and Conditions of Carriage/Service found at www.ups.com and at UPS service centers. If carriage includes an ultimate destination or stop in a country other than the country of departure, the Convention on the Unification of Certain Rules Relating to International Transportation By Air as amended (Warsaw Convention) or the Montreal Convention may apply and in most cases limits UPS's liability for loss or damage to cargo. Shipments transported partly or solely by road into or from a country that is party to the Convention on the Contract for the International Carriage of Goods By Road (CMR) are subject to the provisions in the CMR notwithstanding any clause to the contrary in the UPS Terms. Except as otherwise governed by such international conventions or other mandatory law, the UPS terms limit UPS's liability for damage, loss or delay of this shipment. There are no stopping places which are agreed upon at the time of tender of the shipment and UPS reserves the right to route the shipment in any way it deems appropriate.

01774006   RRD

Store Number: 977

Elms College Bookstore
291 Springfield Street
Chicopee, MA 01013
(413) 594-5500

9770000008028 - 0008448184   09/22/2021

W00535744

Jalaysia Isaac
291 Springfield Street
Chicopee, MA 01013

Shipping Mode: Ground
Questions about returns or items received, contact the bookstore or customer service at 1-888-279-8008.

ISBN	Title	DueDate
9780809148936	Biblio Data not available	

SEE NOTICE ON REVERSE regarding UPS Terms, and notice of limitation of liability. Where allowed by law, shipper authorizes UPS to act as forwarding agent for export control and customs purposes. If exported from the US, shipper certifies that the commodities, technology or software were exported from the US in accordance with the Export Administration Regulations. Diversion contrary to law is prohibited.
RRD R 0121